02119526

Plant Physiology

The Structure of Plants Explained

D0130144

STRODE'S COLLEGE LIBRARY

Studymates

Algebra: Basic Algebra Explained
Better English
Better French
Better French 2
Better German
Better Spanish
British History 1870-1918
Chemistry: chemistry calculations explained
European History
Genetics
Hitler & Nazi Germany
Lenin, Stalin and Communist Russia
Mathematics for adults
Organic Chemistry
Plant Physiology
Poems to Live By
Poetry
Practical Drama
Shakespeare
Social Anthropology
Study skills
The Academic Essay
The English Reformation
The New Science Teacher's Handbook
The War Poets
Understanding Maths
Warfare

Studymates Writers Guides

Kate Walker's 12-Point Guide to Writing Romance
Starting to Write
Writing Crime Fiction
Writing Historical Fiction
Writing Tv Scripts

Studymates Post-Graduate Guides

Your Masters Thesis
Your PhD Thesis

Many other titles in preparation

Plant Physiology

The Structure of Plants Explained

Dr Edwin Oxlade

Studymates

© 2007 by Edwin Oxlade
additional material © 2007 Studymates Limited.

ISBN: 978-1-84285-048-0

First published in 2007 by Studymates Limited.
PO Box 225, Abergele, LL18 9AY, United Kingdom.

Website: http://www.studymates.co.uk

All rights reserved. No part of this work may be reproduced or stored in an information retrieval system without the express permission of the Publishers given in writing.

The moral right of the author has been asserted.

Typeset by Vikatan Publishing Solutions, Chennai, India
Printed and bound in Great Britain by Baskerville Press

Contents

Preface

Plant physiology may not be one of the more fashionable or glamorous of the sciences, but we neglect it at our peril. Plants are, after all, at the base of all food chains and are the only biological source of energy on this planet. The fossil fuels that we are burning at a rate that will see them exhausted in the relatively near future owe their origin to the photosynthesis of green plants. We are already looking to plants to provide the fuels of the future: ethanol from sugar cane and maize, and bio-diesel from plant oils. We may also find the answer to the problem of increasing greenhouse gases and global warming in the ability of green plants to fix carbon. For example, what if varieties of plant were developed that fixed carbon twice as efficiently as now, or three times, or even more so?

It could be argued that the future of the planet lies in the hands of plant physiologists. This book aims to help, if only in a small way, to ensure that enough people have a sufficient knowledge of all aspects of plant physiology to keep the subject thriving for generations to come. If, at the same time, it assists the reader through school, college and university courses and to pass the required exams it will have proved doubly useful.

To use the book you will need some basic knowledge of physics, chemistry and plant biology but the emphasis has been on trying to keep each topic as simple as possible and avoiding issues that would merely complicate things for the reader. As to who that reader might be: if you are studying plant biology, agriculture, horticulture or forestry or simply have an interest in the way plants work you should find the book helpful.

Dr Edwin Oxlade

Water

One-minute overview

Terrestrial higher plants obtain the water they need by root uptake from the soil. Water moves from the roots to the leaves in the xylem, in response to a water potential gradient. Most of the water taken up by a plant is lost by evaporation (transpiration) and only a small amount is used in growth and photosynthesis.

In this chapter you will learn about:
- the importance of water
- water uptake and transport
- the forces that move water in plants
- the meaning of water potential and factors that affect it
- water relations of plant cells
- stomatal control
- adaptations to life in dry places

The importance of water

- water is the medium for all living processes. In the absence of water there can be no life at all.
- water makes up the largest part of the fresh weight of all plants. A cucumber, for example, is over 90% water.
- water pressure is what supports the non-woody plant body.
- growth in plants requires the full hydration of cells and tissues.
- hydrogen bonding in water is essential for the conformation and function of enzymes.
- water is also the source of hydrogen for the reduction of carbon dioxide in photosynthesis (Ch. 2).

Sources of water

A plant must absorb water from its immediate environment. In regions where cloud, mist and rain are prevalent, the atmosphere can be a reliable source, the water being absorbed through the aerial parts of the plant. For most terrestrial plants, however, the air has a drying effect and water has to be drawn from the ground through the plant's roots.

Transpiration

The loss of water by evaporation from the aerial parts of a plant is known as **transpiration**.

> **Key point**
> Throughout the life of a plant, as much water has to be absorbed as is lost to the air by evaporation (in addition to the small amount retained for growth).

Most transpiration occurs through leaf surfaces: this is the greatest part of the plant's surface area. Although the surface of a leaf is usually covered by a waterproof layer (the **cuticle**), it is riddled with holes through which water vapour can pass. These holes are called **stomata**. They allow gas exchange between the air and the intercellular spaces of the leaf. Without stomata a plant would lose very little water through transpiration but its photosynthetic efficiency would be reduced. For this reason transpiration is a 'necessary evil'.

The pathway of water through a plant

The transpiration stream

As water is lost from the leaves by transpiration there is a continuous passage of water up a plant, the magnitude of which depends on the rate of transpiration. This water movement is called the **transpiration stream**. It has been suggested that the transpiration stream aids the movement of mineral salts from roots to leaves and that evaporation from the leaves has a beneficial cooling effect. Plants are, however, in no way disadvantaged when growing in a saturated atmosphere, with hardly any transpiration stream.

Xylem

Key point
Connecting the leaves, through the stem, to the roots, is a continuous system of fine tubes making up the water conducting system of the plant, the **xylem.**

Xylem has the following features:

- it largely comprises non-living cells with impermeable thickening of the cell walls
- it is continuous throughout the plant and every part connects to every other
- water can pass uninterrupted from one cell or element to an adjacent one
- water exists in the xylem in a continuum in which each water molecule coheres to others and no molecule moves without others moving along with it.

Uptake by roots

The amount of water absorbed by the roots of a plant can be huge. For example a medium sized tree can lose up to 500 litres of water by transpiration in a day. The rate at which a root system can absorb water is directly related to the extent of the root system and to the surface area in contact with the soil. Again, both these things can be almost unbelievably large. The roots of a single four-month-old rye plant were calculated to have a combined length of 623 km and a total surface area of 639 m^2.

Root hairs

These are thin walled extensions of the surface of the epidermal cells near the root tips. A single root tip may have up to 2,500 root hairs per cm^2 and each root hair may be several centimetres long. The net effect of the hairs is to increase the absorbing area of the roots. In the example above, the contribution of root hairs to the total surface area of the root system was estimated to be 402 m^2 (63%).

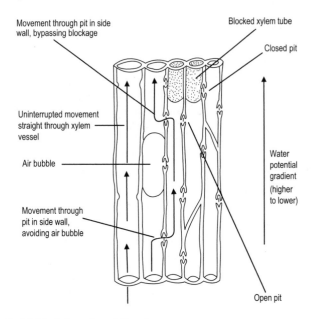

Movement through pit in side wall, bypassing blockage

Blocked xylem tube

Closed pit

Uninterrupted movement straight through xylem vessel

Air bubble

Movement through pit in side wall, avoiding air bubble

Water potential gradient (higher to lower)

Open pit

Fig. 1.1: The Pathway through the xylem

From root surface to xylem

The root surfaces, in particular the root hairs, are in close contact with water in the soil and, unlike the aerial parts of the plant, have no waterproof covering. Water can pass readily, therefore, into the root itself.

Between the surface of the root and the root xylem elements are the living cells of the root cortex and then, separating the cortex from the vascular tissue, a very important girdle of specialised cells called the **endodermis** (fig. 1.2). Water has to pass by all these cells before it reaches the xylem.

Apoplast and Symplast

Movement of water across the root cortex can either be through the living cytoplasm of cells and from cell to cell via **plasmodesmata** or through non-living cellulose cell walls and intercellular spaces. The terms **symplast** and **apoplast** are used to refer to the living and the non-living pathways through plant tissues, respectively.

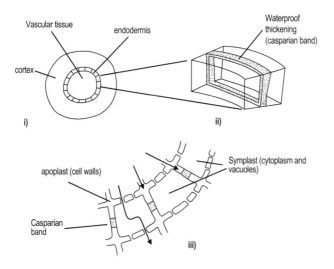

Fig. 1.2:

i) transverse section through root showing position of endodermis.

ii) Single endodermal cell showing ring of waterproof thickening (casparian band) round radial and transverse walls.

iii) Pathway of water through the apoplast is blocked by the casparian band, the only remaining pathway is via the symplast.

The distinction between apoplast and symplast, as far as water transport across root tissues or any other region of living cells in the plant is concerned, is academic. Both pathways are used and there is free exchange of water between them. For mineral uptake and movement, however, the difference is crucial (see Ch. 5).

The endodermis

The importance of the endodermis in roots is that it acts as a barrier to water passing through the apoplast. In order for water to enter the xylem, having passed from the soil and through the root cortex, it has to enter and traverse the living contents of endodermal cells. This device ensures that the contents of the xylem are not directly continuous with the soil solution. Again, although this discontinuity has few implications as far as water is concerned, it is vital to the control of mineral uptake

(Ch. 5). Fig. 1.2 shows how waterproof thickenings of the walls of the endodermis force water to take the symplast route to the xylem.

The mechanism of water movement

Strasburger's experiment

Strasburger's famous experiment of 1891 was to poison a tree and demonstrate that it was still capable of transporting water through its trunk and into every leaf.

> **Key point**
> The movement of water from the roots to the leaves in even the tallest trees is a purely physical process and no living mechanisms need be involved.

The forces for water movement

A number of forces, e.g. pressure, have some part to play in the movement of water in plants. One concept, however, that of **water potential**, is used to bring all these forces under one umbrella.

> **Key point**
> Water always moves in response to a water potential gradient i.e. from higher to lower water potential.

Water potential

> **Key point**
> Water potential is the chemical potential of water in any system compared with that of pure water at the same temperature and at atmospheric pressure.

The value of water potential for pure water is set at zero and this is the standard against which all other water potentials are usually compared. The units of water potential are pressure units (pascals or bars). The symbol for water potential is the Greek letter 'psi' - Ψ.

Understanding the concept

In a survey of perceived difficulty of topics in post -16 level biology, plant water relations was once found to be **the** most difficult.

There are probably two reasons for this.

- The first is that it is a topic that is often treated mathematically, with some difficult formulae made even more confusing because water potential values are invariably negative (remember that the water potential of pure water is set at zero).
- The other reason is that it is a rather abstract concept.

> **Study tip**
> Think of water potential as the 'availability' of water in an object, a place or a system. Then remember the golden rule that water always passes from higher to lower water potential (from wetter to less wet).
> For example, if you wash your hands and then dry them on a dry towel, water passes from the hands to the towel. The force for the transfer of the water is generated by the difference in water potential; hands higher than towel. If someone with dry hands now uses the towel simply to wipe their hands they will find their hands becoming damp. A wet towel has a higher water potential than dry hands.

Whenever water moves in plants the only explanation you need give is that one part has a higher water potential than another. That is the beauty of water potential. It dispenses with the need to break down motive forces into their component parts.

Factors affecting water potential

Usually only pressure, solute concentration and adhesion of water to surfaces are considered in discussion or calculations of water potentials in plants. The contribution of pressure to the water potential of plant tissue is the **pressure potential**, Ψp, the contribution of solutes is the **solute potential, Ψs,**

Factors increasing water potential	Factors decreasing water potential
increasing pressure	decreasing pressure
decreasing solute concentration	increasing solute concentration
	adhesion of water to surfaces
increasing temperature	decreasing temperature
height energy due to gravity	

and that of surfaces to which water tends to adhere is the **matric potential,** Ψm. The sum of these three variables is the water potential of the tissue, Ψ.

> **Key point**
> $\Psi = \Psi s + \Psi p + \Psi m$
>
> **Study tip**
> This is the only formula you will need for calculations of water potential, but beware of two things:
> i) Some values in the equation can be positive and some negative.
> ii) It is impossible to separate the relative contributions of the solute potential and the matric potential, both of which lower the water potential of a cell or tissue. Usually they are considered as one combined potential and given the symbol Ψs.

Water relations of single cells

Osmosis

Osmosis is the diffusion of water from a less concentrated to a more concentrated solution when the two solutions are separated by a barrier that is permeable to water but not to the solute. Such a barrier is called **semipermeable** or **selectively permeable**. The cell membrane is a good example of a semipermeable membrane. Water can diffuse freely through it but solutes cannot. When a cell is immersed in a solution or in pure water, therefore, ideal conditions for osmosis exist. Water can move into or out of the cell without the exchange of either the solute in the immersing solution or any of the solutes in the cell.

Osmotic pressure

Omosis can move water against an opposing force. It can lift water against the force of gravity, for example. It can move water into a cell against the pressure of the cell wall. This force generated by osmosis is referred to as **osmotic pressure.** The maximum osmotic pressure that a solution can generate is equivalent to its solute potential Ψs.

The turgid cell

When a plant cell is fully turgid (i.e. inflated with water until it can take no more) it has a water potential of zero, the same as pure water at the same temperature and pressure. How can this be? The cell still contains solutes and lots of surfaces to which water adheres and might, therefore, be expected to have a negative water potential.

Wall pressure

The reason for this apparent contradiction is that plant cells have a semi elastic cell wall. As the cell fills with water it inflates, like a balloon. The cell wall becomes tight and begins to exert a pressure against the contents of the cell. This pressure is called **wall pressure** and tends to squeeze water out of the cell. In the equation above the pressure potential Ψp represents this cell wall effect and has a **positive** value. It **raises** the water potential of the cell.

When the negative value of the combined solute potential Ψs and matric potential Ψm is equal to the positive value of the pressure potential Ψp they cancel each other out and the water potential of the cell becomes zero. The forces drawing water into the cell are equal to those squeezing it out.

For a fully turgid cell (one which is fully inflated with water):

$\Psi = 0 = (\Psi s + \Psi m)$ (negative) $+ \Psi p$ (positive)

$(\Psi s + \Psi m)$ is numerically equal to Ψp but opposite in sign.

Turgor pressure

To every action there is an equal and opposite reaction (Newton's third law). Wall pressure is the reaction to **turgor pressure** (the force with which the contents of the cell push against the cell wall). So, wall pressure and turgor pressure are equal but opposite consequences of the absorption of water by a cell.

Plasmolysis

A single cell is fully turgid when it is surrounded by pure water. What happens when the water potential of the environment of a cell is itself low?

If a cell is immersed in a solution of lower water potential than that of the cell, water is withdrawn from the cell until the two water potentials equalise. If the solution has a low enough water potential, water will be withdrawn from the cell and the contents of the cell will shrink to such an extent that they no longer fill the space within the cell wall. A cell in this state is said to be **plasmolysed** (fig. 1.3).

A plasmolysed cell generates no turgor pressure and, therefore has no wall pressure. At equilibrium (when water no longer leaves the cell, nor enters it) the water potential of the immersing solution is equal to that of the cell, which is now the sum of the solute potential and the matric potential alone.

Ψimmersing solution = Ψcell = Ψs + Ψm (Ψp = 0)

Fig. 1.3 summarises the water relations of a single cell.

Measuring water potential of plant tissues

Several methods are available for water potential measurement but they all depend on the same principle. If plant tissue is surrounded by a medium (a solution, for example) of known water potential and no movement of water is detected, either into or out of the tissue, then the tissue must have the same water potential as the surrounding medium.

For example:

Dried and weighed pieces of the plant tissue are placed in each of a series of sucrose solutions of increasing concentration

Immersing solutions of increasing concentration from zero
(pure water)

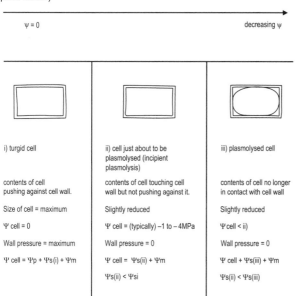

$\psi = 0$ decreasing ψ

i) turgid cell	ii) cell just about to be plasmolysed (incipient plasmolysis)	iii) plasmolysed cell
contents of cell pushing against cell wall.	contents of cell touching cell wall but not pushing against it.	contents of cell no longer in contact with cell wall
Size of cell = maximum	Slightly reduced	Slightly reduced
Ψ cell = 0	Ψ cell = (typically) -1 to -4 MPa	Ψ cell < ii)
Wall pressure = maximum	Wall pressure = 0	Wall pressure = 0
Ψ cell = Ψp + Ψs(i) + Ψm	Ψ cell = Ψs(ii) + Ψm	Ψ cell + Ψs(iii) + Ψm
	Ψs(ii) < Ψsi	Ψs(ii) < Ψs(iii)

The information refers to a single cell immersed in solutions of increasing concentration and left to reach equilibrium (i.e. when water no longer moves either into or out of the cell). At this point the water potential of the cell is equal to that of the immersing solution.

Fig. 1.3: Water relations of a single cell

(usually 0 – 0.5 M will suffice). The pieces are left immersed in their solutions for an hour or two and then removed, dried and reweighed. If they have gained weight it is because they have absorbed water from a solution of higher water potential. If they have lost weight then they were immersed in a solution of lower water potential. The solution in which they neither gained nor lost weight is the one with a water potential equal to that of the plant tissue.

Cohesion theory of water movement

So, how does water reach the top of a tree, maybe over one hundred metres tall? Atmospheric pressure can only raise water to a height of approximately ten metres. That represents the suction power of a vacuum. A tree can suck with ten times this force or more and no living mechanisms are needed to generate the forces involved.

> **Key point**
>
> The theory that is now accepted, with minor modifications, to account for the physical movement of water from root to leaf in plants is called the **cohesion** theory:
>
> - the motive force is the gradient of water potential from air to soil, potentially a force several hundred times atmospheric pressure
> - there is a continuum of water between soil water and leaf cell surfaces
> - in which molecules are held together by cohesive forces.
> - these cohesive forces are extremely strong and give the theory its name
> - the xylem consists of very narrow tubes that assist in maintaining the continuous columns of water in the plant; even if individual columns are broken there are still connections across the xylem via the side walls of xylem elements (see fig. 1.1)
> - transpiration removes water from the top of the plant; cohesion pulls water up from the soil; cohesive forces between water molecules are strong enough to resist the efforts of the transpiration pull to break the water columns
> - when a plant is actively transpiring the water in the xylem is usually under tension (negative pressure).

The control of water movement

Although water movement is brought about by purely physical means, the plant has one controlling system. It can open or close its stomata. When stomata are open transpiration can proceed at a high rate, dependent on the atmospheric conditions, whereas when they are closed transpiration is very much reduced, even at times of potentially high evaporative rates.

The stomatal mechanism

A stoma is a small pore surrounded by two **guard cells**. Opening and closing of the pore is effected by changes in turgor of the guard cells (see fig. 1.4).

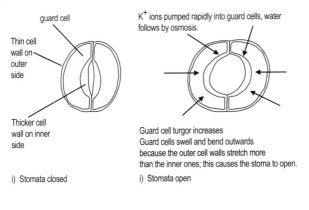

i) Stomata closed

i) Stomata open

Fig. 1.4: Stomatal Mechanism

The pattern of stomatal opening

Usually, (though see Ch. 2, CAM plants), stomata open in the daytime and shut at night. Carbon dioxide, therefore, can diffuse into the leaf when photosynthesis is taking place and transpiration is reduced when photosynthesis ceases. Stomata generally close when the plant has a water deficiency and often there is a period in the middle of the day when stomata close.

Plants in dry places

Given the evaporative power of the atmosphere, the necessity for pathways for the exchange of gases between plant cells and the air that surrounds them, the requirement for plant tissues to be fully hydrated for any growth to take place and the frequent scarcity of water, it is a wonder that plants survive in a terrestrial environment.

Plants can live in a desert by employing one or more of the following strategies:

i) being very efficient at taking up whatever water is available
ii) conserving water
iii) storing water in fleshy tissues
iv) surviving desiccation (being drought hardy)
v) avoiding periods of very low water availability in a dormant state (drought avoidance)

Plants of dry habitats are called **xerophytes**. They often have the following morphological adaptations:

- an extensive root system, able to absorb water from very dry soils
- a thick waxy covering to the stems and leaves
- stomata that are sheltered in grooves or in leaves that roll up or by hairs, or stomata that open only at night (see Ch. 2, CAM plants)
- a low surface area to volume ratio with reduced leaves and fleshy water storage tissue (succulent plants).

Tutorial

Progress questions

1. Define water potential. What factors affect water potential?
2. What are:
   i) turgor pressure
   ii) wall pressure
   iii) solute potential
   iv) matric potential?
   How does each contribute to the water potential of plant tissue?
3. Describe a plasmolysed cell.
4. According to the cohesion theory, how does water reach the top of a tree?
5. How and under what circumstances do stomata open and close? What effect does stomatal closure have on transpiration?

Seminar discussion

1. How is xylem tissue structurally adapted for its water conducting function?
2. Why is transpiration a 'necessary evil'?
3. Discuss the view that dependence on water has been the greatest single force in plant evolution.

Practical assignments

1. Find out the details of Strasburger's 1891 experiment showing that a dead tree still transports water from trunk to leaves.
2. Measure the water potential of potato tuber tissue by means of the method on p. 10. Or, instead of weighing the pieces, cut thin strips 5.0 cm long and re-measure them after immersion in graded sucrose solutions (0.0 – 0.5 M). Draw a graph of change in length of potato strips against water potential of immersing solution and identify a solution in which there is no change in length. This solution has the same water potential as the tissue.

Study tips
1. See p. 8 for an important reminder.
2. If you are calculating water potentials mathematically you will not get confused over positive and negative signs if you keep in mind whether a particular component is forcing water into (negative) or out of (positive) the cells.
3. Older texts will contain a number of out of use terms that are best ignored (e.g. suction pressure, diffusion pressure deficit, etc.).

2 Photosynthesis

One-minute overview

Photosynthesis is the basis of green plant nutrition. The process occurs in chloroplasts and involves the fixation of carbon dioxide into organic molecules and the reduction of these molecules by the hydrogen atoms in water. Subsequent addition of elements, such as nitrogen and phosphorous, also from inorganic sources, enable all the molecules of life to be manufactured. Photosynthesis is powered by light energy absorbed by pigment molecules.

In this chapter you will learn about the:

■ structure and function of chloroplasts
■ three ways in which carbon dioxide is fixed by plants
■ light powered reactions of photosynthesis
■ role of pigments
■ immediate products of photosynthesis.

Photosynthesis – the general picture

A word equation for photosynthesis

Key point
The overall process of photosynthesis can be expressed as follows:
Carbon dioxide + water + light = carbohydrate + oxygen

The scale of photosynthesis

How much photosynthesis occurs worldwide each year? A single seed can grow into a plant weighing several kilograms in a season. Even the dry weight of that plant may be considerable – and it's all organic matter made by photosynthesis from carbon dioxide, water and a few mineral elements. Table 2.1 gives some idea of the global scale of photosynthesis.

Study tip

Do not be tempted to try to balance the word equation above.

You may come across a 'balanced' equation for photosynthesis in your reading, namely:

$$(6CO_2 + 6H_2O = C_6H_{12}O_6 + 6O_2)$$

This is best avoided for two reasons:

i) there is no such reaction –

the pathway from carbon dioxide and water to carbohydrate in photosynthesis is much more complex than this.

ii) The oxygen produced in photosynthesis comes only from water, in which case the equation is **not** balanced: there are six atoms of oxygen in water on the left hand side and six molecules (twelve atoms) of oxygen on the right.

▶
Table 2.1:
Net productivity
through
photosynthesis
of different
ecosystems.
Units are
grams of dry
organic matter
produced
per year per
square metre
and billions of
metric tons per
year

Ecosystem type	Net primary production per unit area (g/m²/yr)	World net primary production (10⁹t/yr)
Tropical rainforest	2,200	37.4
Temperate forest	1,250	15.0
Temperate grassland	600	5.4
Arable land	650	9.1
Freshwater	250	0.5
Marine	150	55.0

A two-stage process

Key point

The reactions of photosynthesis are in two mutually dependent stages:

1. The fixation and reduction of carbon dioxide.
2. The oxidation of water by light energy and the generation of ATP and reducing power.

These two stages are often referred to as the **dark** and **light reactions** or the **light independent** and **light dependent reactions** of photosynthesis. But, in reality, neither stage of photosynthesis proceeds in the absence of light.

The chloroplast

> **Key point**
> All the reactions of photosynthesis take place in chloroplasts. Chloroplasts are liberally scattered throughout those living cells of green plants that have good access to light. Typically a single leaf palisade cell may have up to one hundred chloroplasts.

The structure of a chloroplast is summarised in fig. 2.1.

The internal membranes of the chloroplast, the **thylakoid** membranes, are the sites of the light initiated reactions of photosynthesis (see fig. 2.5) and the **stroma** is where the synthesis reactions themselves take place.

Carbon dioxide fixation

> **Key point**
> The first step in photosynthesis is the absorption of carbon dioxide from the air and its combination with an acceptor molecule so that it becomes 'fixed' into an organic form. There are three known mechanisms or pathways by which this happens:
> - **The C3 pathway**
> - **The C4 pathway**
> - **Crassulacean acid metabolism (CAM)**

All photosynthesising plants use the first of these pathways for the synthesis of the ultimate products of carbon fixation. Those plants that employ either C4 or CAM metabolism do so **in addition** to the C3 route, as a means of fixing carbon dioxide on a temporary basis. The carbon dioxide fixed by either of these two pathways is stored and then released into the C3 pathway.

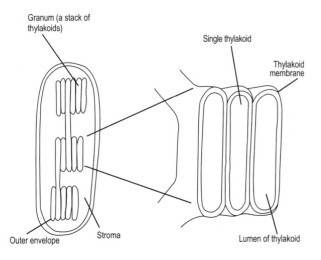

Fig. 2.1: Chloroplast Structure

The C3 pathway

Also known as the **Calvin cycle** or **photosynthetic carbon reduction (PCR) cycle**, this sequence of reactions is the only pathway by which carbon dioxide is permanently fixed in green plants. The cycle attaches a carbon dioxide molecule to a 5-carbon sugar to produce two molecules of a 3-carbon sugar. These molecules are reduced using hydrogen and ATP from the light induced splitting of water (the products of the so called light reactions) and the 5-carbon acceptor molecule is regenerated. All this happens in the stroma of chloroplasts (see fig. 2.2).

Why a cycle?

A number of metabolic pathways are cycles, that is they have no beginning or end but simply go round and round, constantly regenerating their component reactants. The PCR cycle is a good example. The main advantage of a cycle is that there is no need for intermediates to be synthesised by any other pathway. E.g. the carbon dioxide acceptor, ribulose bisphosphate, is made by the cycle itself and need not be supplied from elsewhere. As each molecule of RuBP is used up by combination with carbon dioxide, so another is made by

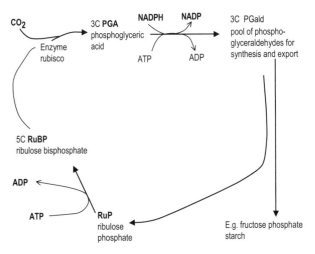

Fig. 2.2: The photosynthetic carbon reduction (PCR) cycle

the cycle to replace it. As long as the cycle is maintained there will always be an acceptor molecule for carbon dioxide.

Input and output

For each turn of the cycle the input is one molecule of carbon dioxide. It follows, therefore, that the net carbon output for a single cycle can only be a single carbon atom. Since the usual product of the PCR cycle is a 3-carbon sugar, three turns of the cycle are required for the synthesis of one such molecule.

The need for NADPH and ATP

The PCR cycle cannot reduce carbon dioxide, nor regenerate RuBP without the input of energy in the form of ATP, and reducing power in the form of the reduced form of the compound **nicotinamide adenine dinucleotide phosphate (NADPH)**. Both these are products of the light reactions of photosynthesis. This explains why the PCR cycle cannot continue in darkness. In the absence of light the cycle quickly runs out of ATP and NADPH and grinds to a halt.

Rubisco

The enzyme that catalyses the reaction joining carbon dioxide to RuBP is **ribulose-bisphosphate carboxylase** or **rubisco** for short.

$$\text{RuBP} + CO_2 + \text{rubisco} = \text{(transient 6C compound)}$$
$$= \text{2PGA (phospho-glycerate)}$$

Rubisco is estimated to be the most abundant protein on earth and is in such high concentrations in the stroma of chloroplasts that it comprises about half of all the soluble protein in a leaf. It is an example of a light activated enzyme, which is another reason why describing the PCR cycle as the 'dark' reactions of photosynthesis is misleading.

Summary of the PCR cycle

In terms of the net product, the fixation of carbon dioxide and the usage of ATP and NADPH the cycle can be summarised:

$$\text{3RuBP} + \text{3}CO_2 + \text{6NADPH} + \text{9ATP} = \text{3RuBP} + \text{6NADP}$$
$$+ \text{9ADP} + \text{GaldP}$$

- this summary represents **three** turns of the cycle
- RuBP is conserved, i.e. regenerated by the cycle
- one molecule of a three carbon compound (glyceraldehyde phosphate, GaldP) is the net product of three turns of the cycle and can be exported from the chloroplast
- NADPH is converted to NADP and ATP to ADP; both these products are required by the light reactions of photosynthesis

The C4 pathway

C4 plants are so called because the first detectable product of carbon dioxide fixation is not a 3-carbon compound as in C3 plants but the 4-carbon acid, **oxaloacetate**. Moreover the fixation of carbon dioxide into this compound occurs in the cytosol of photosynthetic cells, not in the chloroplasts. The substrate that combines with CO_2 is **phosphoenol pyruvate (PEP)** and the enzyme that catalyses the reaction is **PEP carboxylase**.

$$\text{PEP} + CO_2 + \text{PEP carboxylase} = \text{oxaloacetate}$$

Study tip

Organic acids can be referred to either as acids e.g. oxaloacetic acid, malic acid etc. or as the ion: oxaloacetate, malate etc. Treat these alternatives as the same.

The fate of oxaloacetate

The oxaloacetate formed by the fixation of carbon dioxide in C4 plants can be thought of as a temporary store of carbon rather than a real product of synthesis because its ultimate fate is to be converted back to carbon dioxide and PEP. The carbon dioxide enters the PCR cycle and the PEP returns to its job of fixing carbon dioxide (see fig. 2.3).

It may seem a pointless exercise for a plant to fix carbon dioxide, then to unfix it, only so that it can fix it again! Yet C4 plants, such as maize and sugar cane, have some of the highest photosynthetic rates of any plants, especially under hot, dry conditions and high light intensity. One reason is that transferring carbon dioxide from a site of

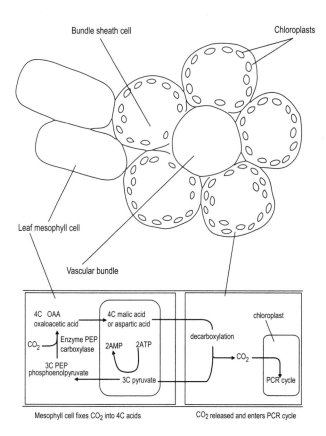

Fig. 2.3: C4 pathway and Kranz anatomy

fixation to a site of reduction and synthesis produces much higher concentrations of the gas in solution in chloroplasts and, therefore much higher rates of reaction. High concentrations of carbon dioxide also suppress photorespiration (see p. 44) and the concomitant loss of fixed carbon.

Energy cost

The advantages of the C4 system do not come free. For every molecule of carbon dioxide assimilated two extra molecules of ATP are required. They are used in the regeneration of the carbon dioxide acceptor PEP.

Kranz anatomy

C4 plants are characterised by a partitioning of the PEP carboxylation reaction and the PCR cycle into two distinct types of cell (**Kranz anatomy** - see fig. 2.3). Carbon dioxide is fixed in the cytoplasm of leaf mesophyll cells, while the PCR cycle takes place in the chloroplasts of cells that surround the veins of the leaf, called **bundle sheath cells** (bundle refers to the vascular bundle i.e. vein). These bundle sheath cells have large numbers of chloroplasts and can be seen in the intact leaf as dark green stripes.

CAM plants

Plants with Crassulacean acid metabolism (CAM) share with C4 plants the ability to fix carbon dioxide into 4-carbon acids (usually malic acid, which is then stored in the cell vacuole) and do so by means of the same cytoplasmic reaction, the uptake of Carbon dioxide by PEP to form oxaloacetate. The term CAM comes from the fact that the pathway was first established in members of the family *Crassulaceae*. CAM plants are almost exclusively succulent plants of dry habitats.

The fixation of carbon dioxide in CAM plants occurs predominantly at night. The plants' stomata open at night; then, during the day, the stomata close and the accumulated malate releases its fixed carbon dioxide to the chloroplasts

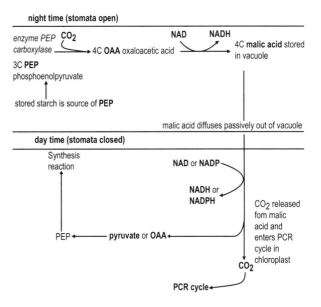

Fig. 2.4: CAM pathway

and the PCR cycle (fig. 2.4). Daytime stomatal closure, conserves water (see Ch. 1).

How are C4 and CAM different?

Two things distinguish CAM from C4. metabolism:

i) CAM plants, in contrast to C4 plants, do not have two separate cell sites for carbon dioxide fixation and the PCR cycle: both occur in the same cell, the former in the cytosol, the latter in the chloroplasts.

ii) In CAM plants the carbon dioxide acceptor, PEP, is not recycled as it is in C4 plants but is derived from the cell's stored carbohydrate.

Light reactions of photosynthesis

From light energy to chemical energy

Key point

Photosynthesis transfers the energy in light to chemical potential energy in organic molecules.

25

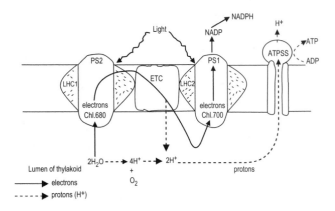

Fig. 2.5: The light reactions of photosynthesis
LHC1, LHC2 = light harvesting complexes for photosystems 1 & 2 (PS1, PS2)
ETC = molecules associated with electron transport chain
ATPSS = ATP synthesising system
Chl.680 = chlorophyll with an absorption peak at 680 nm
Chl.700 = chlorophyll with an absorption peak at 700 nm
    The diagram shows the pathway for electron transport in the thylakoid membrane, electrons passing from water to NADPH via two photosystems and a number of electron carrier molecules. In the process protons accumulate on the lumen side of the membrane and ATP is synthesised as they flow back across the membrane. Light absorbed by pigments in the light harvesting complexes powers the process.

The first step in this transfer is the absorption of light by pigments such as chlorophyll. The end products of the light reactions are ATP and NADPH (see fig. 2.5).

Photosystems and the role of pigments

In the thylakoid membranes of chloroplasts there are aggregations of pigment molecules and associated proteins forming parts of complexes known as **photosystems**. The job of the pigments is to gather light, transform its energy into electro-chemical energy and initiate chemical reactions. Only very few of the pigment molecules in a photosystem are directly linked to the chemical processes of the light reactions. Most are there to absorb as much light as possible and pass its energy on to those chlorophyll molecules that do initiate photochemical reactions; they are called **accessory pigments**. Carotenoids are accessory pigments and the bulk of the chlorophyll in chloroplasts is accessory chlorophyll. It is also referred to as **antenna chlorophyll**.

Energy transfer between pigments can only be from the pigment with the lower peak absorbance wavelength to the one that absorbs most strongly at a higher wavelength. Accessory pigments, therefore, always have absorption peaks at a wavelength less than that of chlorophyll a 680.

Electron transport

When a pigment molecule absorbs a photon of light an electron within the molecule is raised to a higher energy state. The electron is said to be **excited**. In this state the electron can be lost from the pigment and accepted by another molecule – an electron acceptor. This is the basis of a photochemical reaction.

In the light reactions of photosynthesis, chlorophyll passes electrons to acceptor molecules which, in turn, pass them on to other molecules and so on in a chain-like sequence referred to as **photosynthetic electron transport**. In the process the energy in the electron is used to manufacture ATP and, ultimately to reduce NADP.

The end of the chain, the final electron acceptor is NADP (though see non-cyclic photophosphorylation, p. 28) and the beginning, the first electron donor, is not chlorophyll but **water**. When chlorophyll loses light-excited electrons, they are replaced by electrons from water. This releases hydrogen ions (protons) from the water and oxygen, the by-product of the light reactions, is produced.

$$4H_2O = 4H^+ + 4OH^- = 4H^+ + 4 \text{ electrons} + O_2 + 2H_2O$$

or, summarising: * $2H_2O = 4H^+ + 4 \text{ electrons} + O_2$

Redox reactions

The light reactions of photosynthesis produce reducing power (NADPH). They do this by transferring electrons. The addition of electrons is equivalent to the addition of hydrogen and is therefore reduction. NADP, for example is reduced in the light reactions of photosynthesis because it accepts an electron. The resulting negative charge causes it to pick up a hydrogen ion to become NADPH or **reduced NADP.**

Whenever electrons are accepted by one molecule they must have come from another. The molecule that loses electrons is **oxidised.** So, every reduction reaction is also an oxidation. Such reactions are called **redox** reactions. The electron transport system is a series of redox reactions (see also Ch. 3).

Two photosystems

The energy of one photon of light (one quantum of energy) is not enough to send an electron all the way from water to NADP. This became evident when it was discovered that a minimum of **eight** quanta of light energy are required to produce one molecule of oxygen in photosynthesis rather than the four predicted by the equation above* (one quantum releases one electron). Two photosystems are involved in the transport of electrons (see fig. 2.5), called PS1 and PS2. PS2 contains a type of chlorophyll that absorbs light of wavelength 680nm most strongly and PS1 contains chlorophyll of peak absorption at 700nm wavelength. An electron is doubly energised, therefore, in passing through the two photosystems. One thing to note is that the two photosystems are in the wrong order. An electron from water goes first to PS2 and then to PS1.

ATP synthesis

In addition to reducing NADP the transport of electrons provides energy for the synthesis of ATP. The mechanism of ATP synthesis, according to Mitchell's generally accepted **chemiosmotic hypothesis,** relies on three things:

1. a membrane which is impermeable to protons (hydrogen ions) and isolates two regions, one on either side of the membrane,
2. a proton pump which transfers protons from one side of the membrane to the other and produces a proton gradient across the membrane,
3. channels in the membrane which allow protons to pass back in the direction of the proton gradient (i.e. in the

opposite direction to the operation of the proton pump); these channels are the sites of ATP synthesis.

See fig. 2.5 for the basis of the chemiosmotic hypothesis for ATP synthesis in chloroplasts:

- the thylakoid membrane separates the lumen from the outer (stroma) side
- a build up of protons occurs on the lumen side of the membrane as electrons are lost from water
- a further build up occurs because protons are pumped across the membrane into the lumen by the electron transport system
- protons, driven by the concentration and electrical potential gradient across the membrane, pass back to the stroma via ATP synthase channels.

Cyclic and non-cyclic photophosphorylation

When an electron passes all the way from water to NADP, passing by both photosystems on the way it is a one way or **non-cyclic** process. The synthesis of ATP by this means is therefore called **non-cyclic photophosphorylation.**

To some extent, however, the PS1 and PS2 are independent of each other. An electron discharged from PS1 can sometimes pass, not to NADP but back to the start of the electron transport system that joins PS2 and PS1. The electron is returned to where it started (see fig. 2.6), ATP is synthesised, so the process is called **cyclic photophosphorylation.**

Cyclic photophosphorylation, is not accompanied by reduction of NADP nor the evolution of oxygen. It takes place in addition to non cyclic because the ratio of ATP to NADPH needed to support all the activities of the chloroplast is higher than that produced by non-cyclic photophosphorylation alone.

Action spectra for photosynthesis

Light provides the energy for photosynthesis. But not just any light. Some wavelengths are more effective than others. If the photosynthetic yield (oxygen produced or carbon

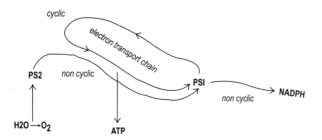

Fig. 2.6: Cyclic and non cyclic photophosphorylation
Lines show pathway of electrons in non cyclic and cyclic photo-phosphorylation.

In non cyclic photophosphorylation an electron starts from PS2 and travels all the way to NADPH.

In cyclic photophosphorylation an electron starts from PSI travels down the electron transport chain and back to PSI. ATP is synthesised but NADPH is not produced, nor is oxygen.

dioxide fixed) is measured for different single wavelengths of light and a graph is plotted, the result is what is known as an **action spectrum** for photosynthesis (fig. 2.7).

Although action spectra for photosynthesis for different species vary, there are general features shared by all green plants (not including red algae and other non-green photosynthetic organisms).

- all wavelengths of light within the visible spectrum (400 nm – 700 nm) are effective in photosynthesis
- red light (approx 600 nm – 660 nm) is most effective
- blue light (approx 450 nm) is the next most effective
- green light is the least effective.

Absorption spectra

An absorption spectrum shows how much light energy is absorbed by a part of a plant, or by a pigment, at single wavelengths across the spectral range. If the absorption spectrum for a pigment mimics the action spectrum for any process, this is good evidence for the involvement of that pigment in the process. You can see (fig. 2.7) that absorption spectra for chlorophylls and carotenoids, like action spectra for photosynthesis show peaks in the blue and red regions. The only puzzle is the relatively

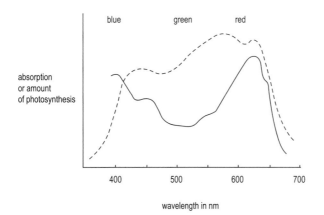

blue   green   red

absorption
or amount
of photosynthesis

400   500   600   700

wavelength in nm

Fig. 2.7: Action Spectrum for photosynthesis and absorption spectrum of a green leaf
The graphs show (dotted line) a composite action spectrum for photosynthesis of a number of crop plants and (solid line) an absorption spectrum for a typical green leaf containing chlorophylls and carotenoids.

high levels of photosynthetic activity brought about by green light.

Photosynthetic products

Organic matter is first stabilised in photosynthetic cells either as starch or sucrose. Sucrose is the form in which most organic matter is translocated in plants (see Ch. 6.).

Both starch and sucrose are synthesised from the pool of 3C sugars produced by the PCR cycle. Starch is made in the chloroplast itself whereas sucrose is made in the cytosol. To some extent, therefore, the balance between sucrose and starch synthesis is a competitive one. Both synthesis pathways use the same raw materials.

The carbon skeletons of all a plant's organic constituents can be traced back to photosynthesis. The modification of these skeletons and the addition of other elements can take place almost anywhere in the plant. In the next chapter, for example, you will see how the metabolic pathways associated with respiration can provide starting points for synthesis. But remember that the substrates for respiration come from photosynthesis.

Tutorial

Progress questions

1. The reactions of photosynthesis are in two mutually dependent stages. What are they and where do they take place?
2. How is carbon dioxide fixed in:
   - i) C3 plants
   - ii) C4 plants
   - iii) CAM plants?
3. What part do pigments play in photosynthesis?
4. What is the role of electron transport in photosynthesis?
5. Oxygen is a by-product of photosynthesis. Where does it come from?
6. What are the essential features of the chemiosmotic hypothesis for ATP synthesis and how do they apply in the case of photosynthetic ATP production?

Seminar discussion

1. Is the term 'dark reactions' a misnomer?
2. Discuss the advantages and disadvantages of C4 and CAM metabolism compared with that of C3 plants.
3. To what extent does photosynthesis control the amount of carbon dioxide in the atmosphere. Is this the answer to global warming?

Practical assignment

1. Refer to the structure of a leaf and identify those features that aid photosynthesis by ensuring:
   - i) the supply of carbon dioxide
   - ii) efficient light absorption
   - iii) the supply of water and mineral salts
   - iv) storage and export of photosynthetic products

One-minute overview

Respiration releases the chemical potential energy in organic molecules by oxidising them to carbon dioxide and water and, in the process, making ATP. ATP is a molecule that can power energy-requiring activities in plants by linking them to its own breakdown. Although some ATP can be produced in the absence of oxygen, aerobic conditions are essential for releasing all the available energy in respiratory substrates.

In this chapter you will learn about:
- the need for energy
- the important role of ATP in plant function
- the breakdown of organic substrates and the consequent synthesis of ATP
- the importance of oxygen
- respiratory pathways as sources of molecules for synthesis.

The need for energy

All living processes need energy. The very organisation and stability of living systems appears to defy the second law of thermodynamics '*the capacity of an isolated system to do work continually decreases*' – unless there is a net input of energy. And yet work is constantly being done by cells in synthesis reactions, in moving solutes against concentration and electrical potential gradients and in a host of other activities. There must be an input of energy.

For example, respiration supplies all the energy needs in all parts of the root of a plant, in all non-green cells and in all cells, including chloroplast bearing cells, when it is dark. Even in green cells in the light, respiration still goes on.

> **Key point**
> While light energy is, ultimately, the only source of energy for green plants respiration is the supplier of energy whenever and wherever light is unavailable and wherever the apparatus for the energy gathering reactions of photosynthesis are absent.

Respiration and photosynthesis compared

In many respects respiration is the opposite of photosynthesis.

- respiration oxidises organic molecules with the release of energy – photosynthesis reduces carbon dioxide to form organic molecules and requires an input of energy
- respiration uses oxygen – photosynthesis produces oxygen
- the products of respiration are carbon dioxide and water – these are the starting points for photosynthesis.

Don't think of respiration as the **reverse** of photosynthesis, except in the general sense that the former is a **catabolic** process (breaking down) and the latter is **anabolic** (building up). The reaction pathways in each case are quite different. Respiration takes place in the cytosol and mitochondria of all cells whereas photosynthesis only occurs in chloroplasts and only in cells that contain them.

> **Key point**
> At some stage both respiration and photosynthesis synthesise ATP and most or all of this ATP is the product of electron transport.

ATP

It would be useful at this point to look at the role of ATP in metabolism. ATP is often referred to as a 'high energy' molecule, 'energy rich' or as being the 'energy currency' of the cell. This is shorthand for the fact that the hydrolysis of ATP is energetically highly favourable in the conditions that exist in cells. The reaction....

ATP + H_2O = ADP + Pi (inorganic phosphate) …..
…….has a very large standard free energy change (see Ch. 4).
In other words it is accompanied by the release of a lot of energy. Furthermore the reaction reaches equilibrium only when a very low concentration of ATP is left. So the breakdown of ATP in cells is always going to be favoured and with it will come energy for those processes that require it.

Conversely the synthesis of ATP from ADP and inorganic phosphate is not energetically favoured and can only happen if energy is supplied. We have seen that, in electron transport in photosynthesis this energy comes initially from light but ultimately from the movement of protons across the thylakoid membrane down a concentration gradient. In respiration chemiosmotic generation of ATP also occurs but the original source of energy is the potential chemical energy of organic molecules, released when the molecules are broken down.

ATP acts in living cells as a link between sites where it is made using an energy source and places where energy is required.

Key point
In simple terms ATP takes energy from where it is available to where it is needed.

Substrates for respiration

Almost any organic molecule can be broken down in respiration. By far the majority of photoassimilated carbon in plants, however, is translocated as sucrose. Sucrose represents an energy store, transported from photosynthetic tissue to those parts of the plant that have no source of energy except respiration. It may be stored as starch. It may have originated from stored starch. But the ultimate fate of most of it will be conversion to hexose (6C) sugars and its entry into the metabolic pathways associated with respiration. Much of it will eventually be oxidised completely to carbon dioxide and water.

For convenience, therefore, it will be assumed that the pathways about to be described start with the input of a **hexose sugar**, namely glucose or fructose. Don't forget that there are many other molecules that can be metabolised via these pathways and many different places for them to enter.

Glycolysis

One route leading towards the pathway to the complete oxidation of hexoses is called **glycolysis**. Glycolysis is the sequence of reactions that convert **fructose bisphosphate** (6C) into the three carbon acid **pyruvate**.

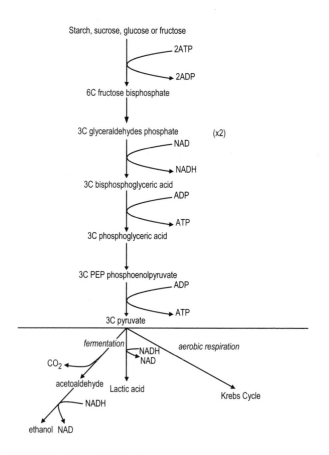

Fig. 3.1: Glycolysis and the fate of pyruvate

The pathway for glycolysis is summarised in fig. 3.1.

- all these reactions occur in the cytosol of cells
- fructose bisphosphate can be derived from starch, fructose or glucose
- the two phosphate groups in fructose bisphosphate come from the breakdown of two molecules of ATP
- there is therefore an energy input (2ATP per hexose) in the production of pyruvate
- two reactions in the glycolytic pathway are energetic enough in themselves to be linked to ATP synthesis (see diagram)
- a total of four molecules of ATP are formed per hexose by this means
- hydrogen is removed from glyceraldehydes by the hydrogen carrier **nicotinamide dinucleotide, NAD** (Note: not NADP, as in photosynthesis but a very similar compound with a similar job)
- potentially, if the NADH formed by dehydrogenation of glyceraldehydes enters a mitochondrion, this is a source of a further four ATP molecules per hexose via electron transport and oxidative phosphorylation (see p. 43)
- the net production of ATP by glycolysis, starting from glucose and assuming NADH is oxidised in the mitochondria is six molecules ATP per hexose molecule
- pyruvate, the end product of gycolysis, can either enter mitochondria and be completely oxidised by means of the Krebs cycle (see p. 38) or be converted to ethanol or, sometimes, lactic acid (see fermentation).

Pentose phosphate pathway

An alternative route by which hexoses can be metabolised in the cytosol is called the **pentose phosphate pathway** (fig. 3.2).

This pathway shares some of its intermediates with glycolysis; consequently a hexose molecule starting down the pentose phosphate route can find itself, or part of itself, then entering the glycolysis pathway to pyruvate. Conversely, molecules may transfer from glycolysis to the pentose phosphate route.

There are good reasons for there being two metabolic pathways for the breakdown of hexoses in the cytosol.

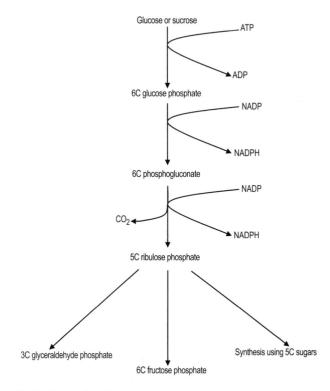

Fig. 3.2: Pentose phosphate pathway

- The pentose phosphate pathway produces NADPH, not NADH as does glycolysis. NADPH is specifically required as the electron donor for some reductive biosynthetic reactions such as in the synthesis of fatty acids. NADH cannot substitute
- Some of the intermediates of the pentose phosphate pathway are precursors for the synthesis of vital organic molecules, such as nucleic acids and lignin
- Synthesis and breakdown can occur in the cytosol simultaneously and with limited competition between them only because there are two separate pathways. For example NADPH produced by the pentose phosphate pathway can be used in synthesis while NADH is oxidised in mitochondria (see below).

Fermentation

In the presence of oxygen, pyruvate is normally passed into the mitochondria where it is completely oxidised. In the absence of oxygen it is converted to ethanol or, less commonly in plants, lactic acid. The conversion of a hexose sugar via glycolysis and pyruvate to ethanol or lactic acid is known as **fermentation**. A limited amount of energy is fixed into ATP and, in the case of ethanolic fermentation, carbon dioxide is given off.

$$C_6H_{12}O_6 = 2C_2H_5OH + 2CO_2 + 2ATP$$

In higher plants fermentation is only an emergency measure to provide energy in the absence of oxygen, as, for example, in roots when the soil is flooded. It cannot proceed for long as both ethanol and lactic acid are harmful products.

Recycling of NAD

Why, in the absence of oxygen, does a plant cell not simply accumulate and store pyruvate? The answer is that it could not do so, because it would very quickly run out of NAD to keep the reactions of glycolysis going. The supply of NAD can only be maintained by the removal of hydrogen from NADH. It is vital that both NAD and NADH are constantly recycled. You will notice in the scheme for glycolysis and fermentation (fig. 3.1) that the conversion of pyruvate to both ethanol and lactic acid uses NADH and regenerates NAD.

Krebs cycle

The **Krebs cycle** (named after Sir Hans Krebs who elucidated it), also called the **citric acid cycle** or **tricarboxylic acid** (**TCA**) cycle, is the sequence of reactions by which

Hans Krebs (1900-1981). He studied medicine at the universities of Göttingen, Freiburg-im-Breisgau, and Berlin. He obtained his Ph.D. from the University of Hamburg in 1925

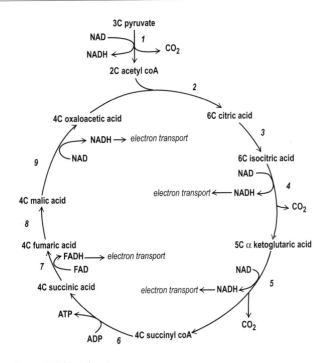

Fig. 3.3: TCA (Krebs) cycle

pyruvate is completely oxidised to carbon dioxide and water (fig. 3.3).

Ultimately this oxidation generates 15 molecules of ATP per pyruvate oxidised. Remembering that two pyruvates come from each hexose molecule that goes down the glycolysis pathway and that glycolysis itself generates 6 ATP molecules per hexose, the total production of ATP from the complete oxidation of one hexose molecule is 36 ATP's or eighteen times what is produced from fermentation.

The importance of oxygen

> **Key point**
> Because aerobic respiration via the TCA cycle yields so much more ATP than fermentation it is extremely beneficial, even essential, for the tissues of a plant to have a good oxygen supply.

Air spaces between cells aid the diffusion of oxygen to the tissues but factors such as compacted soil and the presence of water reduce the availability of oxygen. This is why root growth and mineral uptake (mineral uptake is an energy requiring process – see Ch. 5) are better in soils with an open structure and poor in wet and compacted soils. The aerial parts of a plant don't suffer from lack of oxygen to the same extent.

Mitochondria

> **Key point**
> All the reactions of the Krebs cycle occur in organelles called **mitochondria**.

Like chloroplasts, mitochondria have:

- a relatively permeable outer membrane separating the contents of the mitochondrion from the cytosol (cf. the chloroplast outer membrane)
- a highly folded and selectively permeable inner membrane which has distinct inward and outward facing sides (cf. the thylakoid membranes of chloroplasts)
- a matrix which is completely enclosed by the inner membrane (cf. the chloroplast thylakoid lumen)
- an inter-membrane space (cf. stroma of chloroplast).

Mitochondria, sometimes called the 'power houses' of the cell, are found in greatest numbers in cells which are actively

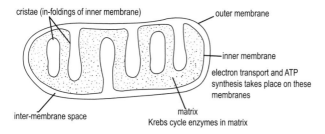

Fig. 3.4: Structure of a mitochondrion

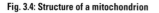

engaged in energy requiring processes such as secretion and solute transfer.

The fate of pyruvate

Before pyruvate can enter the reaction sequence outlined in fig. 3.3 it has to pass from the cytosol through both outer and inner membranes of a mitochondrion. This is because, with one exception, all the enzymes of the Krebs cycle are located in the mitochondrial matrix.

Pyruvate is not itself a component of the Krebs cycle. Before any part of it can enter the cycle it is converted to a 2C compound, **acetyl coenzyme A**, with the loss of carbon dioxide. Acetyl co-A is the entry point for carbon from glycolysis into the cycle itself.

Notes on the cycle

- acetyl co-A enters the cycle by being picked up by oxaloacetic acid, a 4C compound. It is essential, therefore, that oxaloacetic acid is regenerated at each turn of the cycle – which, as you will see from the figure, is exactly what happens
- at two points in the cycle, carbon dioxide is lost. Added to the carbon dioxide lost in the conversion of pyruvate to acetyl co-A this accounts for the three carbon atoms in pyruvate; i.e. pyruvate is completely degraded by one turn of the cycle
- one reaction (reaction 6) is energetic enough by itself to lead to the production of one molecule of ATP
- three reactions (4, 5 and 9) reduce the electron acceptor NAD and produce NADH. This leads to the production of ATP by electron transport
- don't forget that NADH is also produced in the conversion of pyruvate to acetyl co-A
- one reaction (7) produces the related electron donor **FADH$_2$ (flavin adenine dinucleotide)**, another source of ATP via electron transport. (Alternatively the reduced substrate from reaction 7 is **ubiquinol** rather than FADH$_2$ – this is because of the transient nature of FADH$_2$)

- finally the cycle regenerates oxaloacetic acid, ready to pick up another acetyl co-A.

Study tip
read Ch. 2. again – Why a cycle?

Oxidative phosphorylation

The source of most of the ATP from respiration is electron transport. Electrons pass from the electron donors NADH and FADH2 (or **ubiquinol** – see above) through a series of electron carrier molecules to the ultimate electron acceptor, which is oxygen. Water is formed and ATP is generated.

$$NADH + O_2 + ADP + Pi = H_2O + NAD + ATP$$

The process is basically the same as photosynthetic electron transport and the generation of ATP by this means,

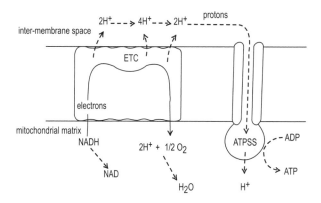

Fig 3.5: Oxidative phosphorylation – electron transport
ETC = molecules associated with electron transport chain
ATPSS = ATP synthesising system
    The diagram shows the pathway for the transport of electrons from NADH to oxygen in the mitochondrial membranes. As a result of the process protons are accumulated on the outer side of the membrane, in the inter-membrane space, and ATP is synthesised as they flow back to the mitochondrial matrix. Compare this diagram with fig. 2.5.

because oxygen is used, is called **oxidative phosphorylation** (cf. photophosphorylation).

The complexes of molecules through which electrons are passed in oxidative phosphorylation are located in the inner membranes of the mitochondria. ATP is synthesised using the potential of a proton gradient established across the membrane, as in photophosphorylation and according to the same chemiosmotic theory (see fig. 3.5).

Photorespiration

In C3 plants (see Ch. 2) the rate of respiration in leaves is actually higher in light than in darkness. The explanation lies in the existence of a process known as **photorespiration,** which is light dependent and which evolves carbon dioxide. Photorespiration causes the breakdown of some of the products of photosynthesis, almost immediately they are formed. The breakdown is by a mechanism unrelated to glycolysis and the Krebs cycle.

Ribulose bisphosphate oxygenase

The enzyme that fixes carbon dioxide in photosynthesis, ribulose bisphosphate carboxylase or rubisco has a dual ability. As well as catalysing the carboxylation of ribulose bisphosphate, it also catalyses the oxygenation of the same compound – one enzyme controlling two reactions.

O_2 + RuBP (5C) + RuBP oxygenase
= phosphoglycerate (3C) + phosphoglycolate (2C)

This reaction is the first step in photorespiration. The PGA can be metabolised via the PCR cycle while the phosphoglycolate enters the photorespiratory cycle and some of its carbon is eventually returned to the chloroplast for synthesis reactions, though some is still lost as carbon dioxide (fig. 3.6).

The dual nature of rubisco means that carbon dioxide and oxygen are competing for its attentions and for the substrate, RuBP. This is why oxygen inhibits photosynthesis and why high levels of carbon dioxide stimulate it. It also explains

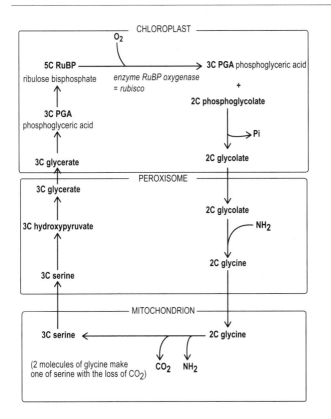

Fig. 3.6: Photorespiration
The scheme for the photorespiratory cycle shown above, also known as the C2 glycolate cycle or photosynthtic carbon oxidation (PCO) cycle is complicated and involves three different cell organelles. It is given here for completeness sake. Things to notice are

i)   the oxidation of RUBP,
ii) the subsequent loss of CO_2 in the mitochondrion but,
iii) the recycling of some of the carbon during the regeneration of RuBP

why C4 plants and CAM plants do not suffer carbon loss through photorespiration – carbon dioxide concentrations are high enough to inhibit the oxidative role of rubisco.

The purpose of photorespiration

The benefit to a plant of photorespiration, a process which seems to undo the good work of photosynthesis and offers no energy gain, is hard to fathom. It may be that:

- rubisco has a dual role simply because it evolved when the earth's atmosphere held very little oxygen and there was no need for it to distinguish between oxygen and carbon dioxide
- given the dual function of rubisco and the inevitable oxygenation of some RuBP, the photorespiratory pathway conserves at least some of the fixed carbon that would otherwise be lost. It does this by recycling glycolate
- some of the intermediates of the photorespiratory cycle may be starting points for biosynthetic pathways
- photorespiration removes excess ATP and NADPH when light levels are very high and photosynthesis is proceeding too fast.

Respiratory Quotient

> **Key point**
> The ratio of carbon dioxide evolved to oxygen used in respiration is called the **respiratory quotient (RQ)**.

Because the RQ for a particular plant tissue or organ represents the sum total of carbon dioxide produced divided by the sum total of oxygen taken up and because both values depend on a number of factors, RQ is an imprecise tool. What can be said is that:

- the RQ for the complete oxidation of a hexose sugar, in the absence of any other reactions involving oxygen or carbon dioxide, is 1.0
- respiration of fats (as in the germination of some seeds) reduces the RQ
- anaerobic respiration (fermentation) increases RQ
- photosynthesis reduces RQ.

Respiration as a source of precursors for biosynthesis

Respiration provides both the energy required for biosynthesis and the carbon skeletons that are its starting point. A few examples will make the point.

- pyruvic acid is a precursor for making the amino acid alanine
- ketoglutaric acid (a Krebs cycle intermediate) can be used to make glutamic acid and other amino acids
- oxaloacetic acid (also Krebs cycle) is used to make aspartic acid, other amino acids and also pyrimidines for nucleic acid synthesis
- phosphoglyceric acid from the glycolysis pathway is a precursor for the glycerol in fats.

There is a danger that when carbon compounds leave a respiratory pathway for synthesis reactions the pathway itself can no longer continue. For example when oxaloacetate is diverted from the Krebs cycle to make aspartic acid it can no longer function as an intermediate of the cycle. It has to be replaced from elsewhere. To this end plant cells are always fixing a certain amount of carbon dioxide into oxaloacetic acid or malic acid using PEP carboxylase (see p).

Only a proportion of the carbon entering respiratory pathways can ever be diverted towards synthesis. Complete oxidation of carbohydrates and liberation of the necessary ATP and NADH or NADPH for synthesis reactions must continue.

Tutorial

Progress questions

1. What is respiration?
2. Where in plants does respiration take place?
3. Summarise the pathways leading to the complete oxidative breakdown of hexose molecules in plant cells.
4. How do plants produce ATP in the absence of both light and oxygen?
5. What is photorespiration?
6. What could explain a respiratory quotient of
    i) less than 1.0
    ii) more than 1.0?

Seminar discussion

1. Since green plants get all their energy from light why do they need respiration?
2. Is respiration the reverse of photosynthesis?

Practical assignments

1. Try making some wine or beer and note:
    i) lack of oxygen
    ii) production of carbon dioxide
    iii) accumulation of ethanol
    iv) breakdown of sugar
    v) growth of yeast.

Study tips

Rather than learn all of the reactions in the pathways associated with respiration be familiar with examples that illustrate general points; e.g. a reaction of the Krebs cycle that removes carbon dioxide and/or that produces NADH, a reaction of glycolysis that produces ATP directly.

4 Enzymes and the Control of Metabolism

One-minute overview

Plant metabolism can be seen as a multitude of single chemical reactions, all of which obey universal physical laws. These individual reactions can only give rise to ordered growth and development due to various control mechanisms. Enzymes are the prime controllers of reactions in cells; regulation of metabolism is mainly by enzyme synthesis, destruction, location and activity.

In this chapter you will learn about:

- the physical laws that metabolic reactions obey
- the effects on reactions of concentrations of reactants and external factors
- the need for activation energy
- enzymes and how they work
- the control of enzyme activity.

The nature of metabolism

The chemical reactions that take place in living systems are known collectively as **metabolism**. Together, these reactions are highly organised, usually into sequences of linked reactions referred to as **metabolic pathways** or **cycles**.

Despite the order and apparent sense of purpose that we associate with living systems, it should never be forgotten that the basis of all metabolism is individual chemical reactions and that these reactions must obey universal physical laws.

Key point
Ultimately the only factors determining every aspect of plant growth and development are the same physical and chemical rules that govern all chemical reactions.

Rules for chemical reactions

Whether a reaction takes place at all, in which direction it will go and how fast it will happen are determined by:

- energy changes and laws of thermodynamics
- effects of concentrations of reactants
- the need for activation energy
- the effects of external factors such as temperature.

Energy changes and thermodynamics

In any reaction energy cannot be lost or gained (first law of thermodynamics) but it can be changed from one form to another. Generally speaking a cell reaction is most likely to happen if chemical energy is lost; that is, if the chemical energy of the products is less than that of the reactants. When a reaction 'loses' energy the energy is released (never really lost) mainly as heat. Reactions of this sort are called **exergonic**. The oxidative breakdown of carbohydrate, for example is an exergonic process.

Carbohydrate + Oxygen = carbon dioxide + water + energy

It will proceed spontaneously and continuously in the direction shown as long as there is enough carbohydrate and oxygen still present. This is what happens when sugar burns. Energy is released as light and heat and the products of the reaction (CO_2 and H_2O) contain less chemical potential energy than the reactants.

Conversely a reaction in which the products contain more energy than the reactants is called **endergonic**. Reactions of this sort need an input of external energy and consequently tend not to happen spontaneously. They are energetically unfavourable.

Key point
Chemical reactions in cells happen because they are energetically favourable.

Free energy changes

The degree to which a reaction is either exergonic or endergonic can be quantified in terms of the so-called **free energy change** for the reaction. This is the difference between the energy of the reactants and that of the products. It can either be expressed as the **actual** change in energy for the conditions and concentrations that apply in a cell, or as a standard energy change for the equilibrium state of a reaction involving molar concentrations (known as **Gibbs standard free energy change**). For metabolic reactions it is the **actual** change in free energy that matters because: i) in cells concentrations of reactants are much less than molar and, ii) reactions rarely reach equilibrium.

If the free energy change for a reaction is negative the reaction is energetically favourable; if it is positive the reaction is not favourable. So, for example, the standard free energy change for the hydrolysis of

ATP is -30 kJ mole^{-1} (kilojoules per mole).

ATP $\rightarrow$ ADP + Pi + 30kJ

This large loss of free energy explains why the hydrolysis of ATP takes place so readily in cells and why ATP is such a useful compound in metabolism (see p. 34).

Linking reactions to drive endergonic processes

If endergonic reactions are unfavourable and tend not to take place in cells how can metabolism include endergonic processes, such as the synthesis of large molecules? The secret lies in linking exergonic and endergonic reactions.

For example the synthesis of glucose phosphate cannot occur in the straightforward way.....

Glucose + phosphate = glucose phosphate

....because the free energy change is $+ 16$kJ mole^{-1} (i.e. an input of energy is needed)

By linking the reaction to the hydrolysis of ATP the synthesis of glucose phosphate becomes exergonic.

ATP + glucose = glucose phosphate + ADP (free energy change = -14kJ mole^{-1}).

Effects of concentration

The thermodynamics of reactions are influenced by the concentrations of the reactants, and, since reactions in cells are theoretically reversible, this means the concentrations of the products as well. The higher the concentrations of reactants the faster the reaction will proceed and the more energetically favourable it becomes. The higher the concentration of the products the slower the reaction becomes in the forward direction.

Substrate concentrations play a large part in controlling metabolism. Often metabolic pathways only continue if the products of individual constituent reactions are quickly used up by the next reaction in the sequence so that their concentrations don't rise too much. Metabolic cycles (e.g. the PCR cycle – see p. 20) are kept going only so long as they regenerate the intermediate compounds and keep the concentrations of these substrates high.

> **Key point**
> One way in which metabolism is controlled is through the concentrations of substrates and products.

Some of the participants in chemical reactions in cells come from the environment. Their concentrations cannot be controlled by the plant but are just as important in determining reaction rates. Carbon dioxide concentration, for example has a major effect on the rate of photosynthesis. Oxygen concentration affects the rate of respiration.

Activation energy

A reaction, the burning of petrol, for example, may be energetically highly favourable but still not happen. This is because it won't start without a once only injection of energy called **activation energy**. Once the activation energy has been supplied the reaction will continue spontaneously with the loss of free energy. When petrol burns in a car engine it is the spark from the spark plug that supplies the activation energy.

Living systems solve the problem of activation energy by means of enzymes.

> **Key point**
> Enzymes lower the necessary activation energy for reactions to an insignificant level.

External factors

Some external factors, like oxygen and carbon dioxide, are themselves reactants in metabolism and affect the rate of reactions through their concentration. Other factors, e.g. pH, affect the chemical environment of a cell and thereby the reactions occurring in it. Then there are physical factors, such as temperature and light, that can influence and control metabolism.

Temperature affects all chemical reactions in the same way: the higher the temperature the faster the reaction (though there is an upper temperature limit for metabolic reactions because enzymes are denatured by heat). The effects of temperature on plant metabolism, growth and development are complex (see Ch. 9) but underlying them is this basic law relating temperature and rates of reactions.

> **Key point**
> Enzymes are what really control metabolism.

Enzymes

This is because they are extremely effective and highly specific **catalysts**. They speed up reactions in cells by colossal amounts, of the order of $10^8 - 10^{20}$ times. With very few exceptions, a single enzyme can only have this effect on one particular reaction. So, every reaction that is part of the whole metabolism of a plant has its very own enzyme. In the presence of this enzyme, the reaction will happen so fast as to be almost instantaneous. In the absence of the right enzyme, the same reaction takes so long that it might as well not be happening at all.

Key point

Reactions in living cells still have to obey the laws of physics and chemistry. An enzyme cannot make an impossible reaction possible: it can only speed it up.

How enzymes work

Enzymes lower the activation energy for a reaction and speed the reaction up. They do this by reacting themselves with their substrate.

Enzymes are complex and infinitely varied protein molecules. They have, within their three dimensional structure, places called **active sites.** The substrate for a particular enzyme is attracted to an active site and combines with it in a very specific way. Because the active site and the substrate fit together so specifically, the mechanism for combination of enzyme and substrate is known as '**lock and key**'. This idea explains why different enzymes control different reactions.

At the active site the reaction takes place and the products are released (fig. 4.1.)

Enzyme control

Given that metabolic reactions will not occur in the absence of the necessary enzymes, control of metabolism is simply a

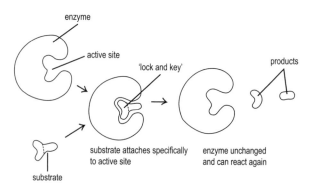

Fig 4.1: Enzyme action

matter of controlling the presence, location and activity of enzymes.

The synthesis of enzymes can be switched on or off at the gene level

Different cells contain different enzymes. Different enzymes appear at different times during a plant's life cycle. This is all part of development and differentiation. For example the enzymes of photosynthesis are found in leaf cells but not in root cells. They appear when a shoot is illuminated but not before.

> **Key point**
> The genes that make enzymes and, therefore, the reactions that these enzymes control, are only switched on at certain times and in certain places.

The rate of enzyme synthesis varies

The rate of a metabolic reaction is affected by the concentration of the relevant enzyme. The faster a cell makes an enzyme, the more of it there will be and the faster the reaction controlled by it will occur.

The location of enzymes can be restricted so that they don't operate wherever their substrate happens to be present

Enzymes are not located randomly in cells. They may be membrane bound or associated with other enzymes and molecules in reaction centres or multi-enzyme complexes. They are often confined to a part of a cell, separated from the rest by cellular membranes. For example the enzymes of the light reactions of photosynthesis are on the thylakoid membranes of the chloroplasts while the dark reaction enzymes are in the stroma. None of these enzymes are found outside the chloroplast.

> **Key point:**
> Compartmentalisation of enzymes allows different parts of cells to have different metabolism.

Activity of enzymes can be turned off by inhibitors

An enzyme may be present but inactivated by an inhibitor. Often the product of a reaction can act as an inhibitor of the enzyme that made it. In this way the useless and wasteful build up of the products of a reaction can be prevented – a mechanism known as **feedback inhibition**.

Enzyme activity can be restricted by the absence of other necessary factors

Enzyme controlled reactions may involve **cofactors** or **coenzymes**. Cofactors are mostly ions (e.g. Ca^{++} and Mg^{++}) or small molecules that promote enzyme activity; coenzymes are larger organic molecules that also help enzymes to function (e.g. the electron/hydrogen carrier NAD). Without the necessary cofactors or coenzymes an enzyme-controlled reaction cannot take place.

Tutorial

Progress questions

1. What factors affect the rate of chemical reactions?
2. What are exergonic and endergonic reactions?
3. Explain the importance in metabolism of the ATP hydrolysis reaction.
4. What do enzymes do and how do they do it?
5. How is the activity of enzymes controlled?

Seminar discussion

1. Do chemical reactions in living and non-living systems follow different rules? Why is the idea that they do so persuasive?

Study tip

1. Learn the names of enzymes that control some of the more important reactions of plant metabolism; e.g. ribulose-bisphosphate carboxylase (p. 21), phosphoenol pyruvate carboxylase (p. 22), amylase (degrades starch), pyruvic acid dehydrogenase and alcohol dehydrogenase (enzymes of fermentation).

5   **Mineral Nutrition**

One-minute overview

Plants require a number of essential elements in addition to carbon, hydrogen and oxygen. The plant absorbs all of these elements as inorganic ions. Mineral uptake is a controlled, selective and active process. The way in which a plant obtains the elements it needs, and the uses to which those elements are put, are referred to as the plant's mineral nutrition.

In this chapter you will learn:

■ which elements are essential for plant growth and why
■ how minerals are taken up by a plant
■ the importance of membranes and active processes in the uptake of mineral ions
■ what happens to mineral ions in plants.

Autotrophic nutrition

Key point
Green plants are entirely **autotrophic** (literally, self-feeding). This means that all the organic materials that make up a plant have come from inorganic sources.

A plant requires no ready-made organic molecules and can live on a diet of nothing but mineral salts, carbon dioxide and water. In addition to carbon, oxygen and hydrogen, plants need a number of chemical elements for their nutrition and all are obtained as inorganic ions dissolved in water. The usually source of these ions is the soil solution. Those elements that are components of a plant's materials (for example nitrogen in amino acids) are first absorbed by the plant as inorganic ions and then enter biosynthetic pathways within living cells, leading to their incorporation into organic molecules.

Essential elements

Dry matter content

Analysis of dry plant material or the ash remaining after plant material is burnt shows the presence of a number of mineral elements (Table 5.1). It does not follow that all these elements are essential for the growth and proper development of the plant. To some extent a plant will absorb any inorganic ions that happen to be present in its environment. In fact the issue of which elements are essential has not been an easy one to resolve and still presents some difficulties.

What is meant by essential?

> **Key point**
> An essential element is one which:
> - is necessary for a plant to complete its life cycle,
> - cannot be replaced by any other element,
> - has a direct action and does not act indirectly by, for example, affecting the uptake of another element,
> - can cure deficiency symptoms that appear when it is absent.

▶
Table 5.1: Some mineral elements present in plant ash and their relative abundance in parts per million

Element	Abundance (ppm)
Potassium	1,000 to 100,000
Calcium	40 to 60,000
Sodium	100 to 50,000
Magnesium	100 to 40,000
Phosphorous	100 to 10,000
Zinc	2 to 500
Barium	5 to 500
Lead	0.01 to 50
Silver	0.01 to 0.5

Note:
i) some essential elements (e.g. nitrogen) are not present in plant ash because they are lost as gases when plant material is burned
ii) some elements are present in plant tissue but are neither essential nor beneficial; they may even be toxic (e.g. lead).

You should also note that, any element that forms part of an essential organic molecule is, by definition, an essential element.

There are still problems in deciding whether some elements really are essential. Sodium, Selenium, Cobalt and Silicon, for example are believed to be essential for some plants but not others. It is possible that other elements are required in such small amounts that analytical techniques are insufficiently sensitive to test their essentiality.

Nevertheless it is possible to list seventeen elements that are agreed to be essential to all plants. Other elements, that are essential only to some species, are referred to as **beneficial elements** (Table 5.2).

Macro and micro elements

For any essential element there is a critical requirement. If the supply of the element to a plant is below this level, the plant will show reduced growth or deficiency symptoms. Above this level there is a range of concentrations that lead to good growth and development. At higher concentrations than these an element may have harmful effects.

There is a huge difference in the relative requirements for the different elements. Those that are required in relatively large amounts are referred to as the **macro elements** and those that are required in very small amounts are the **micro elements** or **trace elements.**

Element	Relative amount needed	Function
Macroelements		
Hydrogen	60,000	component of organic molecules
Carbon	40,000	ditto
Oxygen	30,000	ditto
Nitrogen	1,000	ditto e.g. amino acids

Table 5.2: The functions of the essential and beneficial elements

Continued

Element	Relative amount needed	Function
Potassium	250	enzyme activation and osmoregulation (see stomatal control p. 13)
Calcium	125	membrane function, cell division, enzyme regulation, hormone action
Magnesium	80	component of chlorophyll, enzyme activation
Phosphorous	60	component of organic molecules e.g. sugar phosphates, ATP, NADP, DNA and RNA.
Sulphur	30	component of amino acids and other organic molecules
Microelements		
Chlorine	3.0	oxygen evolution in photosynthesis, osmoregulation,
Boron	2.0	uncertain – probably involved in cell wall structure and cell division
Iron	2.0	component of redox enzymes of photosynthesis and respiration, also required for the synthesis of chlorophyll
Manganese	1.0	enzyme function, in particular in relation to oxygen evolution in photosynthesis
Zinc	0.3	enzyme activation, auxin metabolism
Copper	0.1	enzyme activity e.g. in electron transport
Nickel	0.05	unclear but may be needed for the mobilisation of nitrogen during seed germination

Continued

Element	Relative amount needed	Function
Molybdenum	0.001	component of enzymes associated with nitrogen metabolism
Beneficial elements		
Sodium		C4 and CAM metabolism
Selenium		unclear, maybe a component of enzymes needed by some species only
Silicon		component of cell walls of, especially, grasses
Cobalt		nitrogen fixation in root nodules

Uptake and transport of minerals

To some extent, the movement of minerals into and through a plant follows the same pathway as water (see Ch. 1).

> **Key point**
> It is not true to say that wherever water goes, the minerals dissolved in it can also go.

What divides water movement and the movement of mineral ions is the permeability of cell membranes. Whereas water can move passively through cell membranes into all parts of a plant, mineral ions can only cross living membranes if facilitated or actively transported. The membranes of cells are particularly impermeable to ions and act as barriers to the free movement of minerals. They can **select** mineral ions by allowing them through or, alternatively, **exclude** them by not doing so.

Transport of ions across membranes

- proteins within the membrane act as transporters of ions, bringing about **facilitated diffusion** or **active transport**

- these transport proteins may form **ion channels** or act as **carriers**
- ion channels are not involved in active transport; they are selective, may be open or closed and allow rapid movement of ions across a membrane in response to a signal (e.g. K^+ movement in stomatal guard cells – see p. 13)
- active ion transport is always by means of carrier proteins, metabolic energy is involved, it is unidirectional and leads to ion accumulation
- the proteins that move ions across membranes can recognise specific ions and are therefore selective in their action.

Entry into the root

The water in the soil with all the minerals that are dissolved in it (the soil solution) can enter the apoplast of the root, usually as far as the endodermis. At this point the solution cannot proceed further towards the xylem without passing through a living cell membrane (see p. 5). Selection and exclusion of ions takes place, with the result that the solution inside the xylem differs in composition from that of the soil solution (see Table 5.3). Ions are actively secreted into the xylem from surrounding root cells, leading to a higher concentration of solutes in the xylem than in the soil solution. This secretion of ions into the xylem requires metabolic energy from respiration.

Table 5.3: Typical concentrations of three ions in soil solutions and in xylem sap

Mineral ion	Concn. in soil solution (mM)	Concn. in xylem sap(mM)
Nitrate	< 2	5 – 15
Phosphate	< 0.001	0.2 – 0.7
Potassium	< 1.2	2 – 8

Key point
Concentrations of mineral ions in soil solutions are generally very low but concentrations inside plant cells and in xylem sap are much higher.

Root pressure

One of the forces that helps to move water from the root of a plant to the aerial parts is root pressure. Root pressure can force sap out of the cut end of a stem or up the xylem against the force of gravity to considerable heights. You can now see what causes this force. It is simply the osmotic pressure generated by the difference in osmotic potential between the contents of the xylem and the surrounding soil solution.

Movement in the xylem

Once in the xylem ions move passively with the transpiration stream. This is a quick way for them to reach the leaves and upper parts of the plant by a process that requires no metabolic activity. Most of the xylem, it should be remembered, is dead tissue and, therefore, part of the apoplast.

Unloading of ions from the xylem solution into, for example, leaf cells, is, like the passage of ions through the root endodermis, an active, controlled process.

Accumulation of ions

The concentrations of ions inside plant cells and inside their vacuoles can be very much greater than concentrations outside (Table 5.4). In other words uptake involves **accumulation**. In order to accumulate ions a cell often has to do work and use up energy in the form of ATP. Notice from the table that the degree of accumulation varies for different ions and that some ions are not accumulated at all and indeed may be excluded or even actively extruded from the cell rather than taken up.

The effect of electric charge

For an uncharged solute molecule such as sucrose, a difference in concentration across a membrane is evidence enough for accumulation or exclusion/extrusion since passive diffusion would be expected to equalise the concentrations. For a negatively or positively charged ion, however, accumulation or exclusion/extrusion can only be inferred by considering both the concentration difference and the electric potential difference across the membrane.

Key point

The distribution of mineral ions across plant cell membranes is affected by the electrical charge on the ion and the electrical potential difference across the membrane.

Membrane potentials

Invariably there is an electrical potential difference across a cell membrane, one side being positively charged, the other negatively charged. This is due to a number of factors:

- fixed charges within the cell such as those on protein groups,
- different mobilities of different ions,
- ion pumps and proton pumps acting within the membranes of the cell.

The cytosol of cells is usually negatively charged compared with the outside of the cell and membrane potentials are typically about 100 mv. This means that positively charged ions (cations) will be attracted into the cell and negatively charged ions (anions) will be attracted in the opposite direction. Concentrations of cations can be considerably greater inside a cell than outside without this signifying accumulation by means of active transport. Equally concentration gradients of anions in the opposite direction do not necessarily signify active exclusion or extrusion.

Nernst equation

A calculation will show whether observed concentration differences of any single ion across a membrane are due to active processes or can be explained by passive diffusion alone. The calculation is by means of the **Nernst equation**. The equation adds together the effects of the concentration difference and the electric potential difference across a membrane to give a net chemical potential gradient or **electrochemical gradient** for the ion in question. Only when this gradient is in an unfavourable direction for the movement of the ion (i.e. the ion would naturally tend to be propelled in the opposite direction) can it be inferred that movement of the ion is by an active process.

Applying the Nernst equation

The electric potential difference across the cell membrane is measured and also the concentrations of a particular ion both inside and outside the cell. The Nernst equation is then used to predict the concentration of the ion inside the cell that would be expected by passive transport alone. If the measured and predicted concentrations are very different, then active processes must either be accumulating or excluding/extruding the ion.

Ion	Concentration in external solution (mM)	Concentration in root tissues (mM)	Conclusion
K^+	1.0	75.0	P
Na^+	1.0	8.0	E
NO_3^-	2.0	28	U
SO_4^-	0.25	9.5	U

◀
Table 5.4:
The uptake of some ions by pea roots

The roots were bathed in a mineral solution of known ionic composition and internal concentrations of ions were measured after a period of time. The average electrical potential difference across the cell membranes is 110 mV (inside of cell negative). The final column shows the conclusion, based on application of the Nernst equation, about the mechanism of ion movement: P = passive diffusion, U = active uptake, E = active exclusion

The concentration of potassium ions inside the cells of the root is 75 times that of the external solution, yet there is no evidence for active uptake. Sodium, another cation, is 8 times more concentrated inside the cells and only active **exclusion** will keep it from accumulating even more. On the other hand, Nitrate, an anion, with a concentration difference of 14 times, does have to be taken up actively. Sulphate ions are even more difficult to accumulate inside the cells as they have a double negative charge. The Nernst equation tells us that even if the internal concentration of sulphate were as low as 10^{-4} mM that would still signify active uptake!

Assimilation of mineral ions

What happens to absorbed mineral ions in plant tissues? Some never become incorporated into organic molecules, functioning simply as inorganic ions. Potassium is a good example (see stomatal control Ch. 1). Most essential elements, however, are assimilated into organic form at some point following absorption.

Nitrogen assimilation

Because of the particular importance of nitrogen in the life of green plants its metabolism has been well studied. The pathway for nitrogen assimilation will serve as an example of the way in which minerals are incorporated into a plant's organic systems.

Nitrate reduction

Nitrogen most commonly enters the roots as nitrate ions. The first step to the assimilation of nitrogen is reduction of nitrate to nitrite and then to ammonium ions.

$$NO_3^- \rightarrow NO_2^- \rightarrow NH_4^+$$

This is an energy requiring process. It occurs either in the cytosol and plastids of root cells or in the cytosol and chloroplasts of leaf cells. In some species almost all nitrate reduction occurs in leaves; in other species most takes place in the roots.

Ammonium ions are potentially toxic and are quickly converted into organic form by combination with the 5 carbon amino acid, **glutamic acid**, giving the amide, **glutamine**. Glutamine then becomes the substrate for the synthesis of proteins, nucleic acids and other nitrogen containing organic molecules.

Tutorial

Progress questions

1. What are the seventeen essential elements and why is each of them needed by a plant?
2. What is meant by a 'beneficial element'? Give some examples.
3. Explain why it is easier for a plant to accumulate cations than anions.
4. What happens to mineral ions once inside the plant?

Seminar discussion

1. To what extent is the movement of mineral ions into and through a plant i) a passive process ii) an active process?
2. Why is the root endodermis important in the uptake of mineral ions?

Practical activities

1. Research the techniques used to establish whether different elements are essential for plant growth and the problems involved in reaching a conclusion.
2. Find out how the mineral composition of a plant's soil environment can affect its growth (e.g. calcareous soils, soils contaminated by heavy metals, saline soils, etc.)

> **Study tip**
> Look up the Nernst equation and apply it to the data in Table 5.4. See if you reach the same conclusions.

6 Solute Transport

One-minute overview

Water and mineral ions are transported in the xylem while organic solutes, most commonly sucrose, are transported in the phloem. The direction of phloem transport is from parts of the plant that produce organic substances to places in the plant where they are used. The active loading of solutes into one part of the phloem and their unloading from another, create a pressure difference that causes a mass flow of sap in the phloem sieve tubes.

In this chapter you will learn:

- that translocation of organic solutes takes place in the phloem
- the structure of the phloem
- the concept of sources and sinks
- what types of experimental technique have been used to investigate translocation in the phloem
- the generally accepted mechanism for movement in the phloem.

Solute transport

There are two long distance solute transport systems in vascular plants. The xylem, was covered in Ch. 1. The other is the **phloem**. Let's compare the two:

Xylem	Phloem
largely dead tissue	almost entirely living tissue
contains long thin open tubes called **xylem vessels**	contains long tubes called **phloem sieve tubes**

Continued

Xylem	Phloem
found on the inside of woody stems	found towards the outside
transports water and mineral salts and some organic compounds	transports organic solutes and some minerals
velocity of movement depends on transpiration rate but can be quite fast	velocity relatively slow (about 100 cm h^1)
no metabolic energy required for transport	metabolic energy required to keep system moving
movement is normally in a morphologically upward direction i.e. from root to leaves	movement is in both directions
contents of xylem usually under tension	contents of phloem under pressure
in simple terms solutes are **pulled** through the xylem	solutes are **pushed** through the phloem
the mechanism of transport in the xylem is resolved to the satisfaction of most plant physiologists (see Ch. 1)	the mechanism of phloem transport is less clear, though one mechanism (pressure flow) gets most support
ions are actively loaded into the xylem in the roots and unloaded higher up the plant	organic solutes are actively loaded at sources and unloaded at sinks

Phloem translocation

Key point
The movement of organic solutes in the phloem is called **translocation**.

Sources and sinks

A **source** is a part of a plant that is a net producer of organic solutes. For example, during photosynthesis mature leaves are making more organic material than they are breaking down in respiration. The leaves, in this case, are sources, or exporters of organic compounds.

A **sink** is a part of a plant that is a net importer of organic solutes. Generally speaking, non-photosynthetic and growing parts of a plant are sinks. Take, for example, a developing potato tuber. Organic solutes are being imported into the tuber, where they are used for growth or stored as starch. All the tuber's dry matter has to be made using photo-assimilates produced elsewhere in the plant, because, of course, it cannot photosynthesise itself.

A sink is not always a sink nor a source always a source. A leaf may, in its young, growing phase be a net importer of organic materials (i.e. a sink). A mature potato tuber turns from a sink to a source when it starts to sprout. The nutrients that were once imported into the tuber and stored in its cells are now exported to feed the growing shoots.

> **Key point**
> Translocation of organic solutes is from sources to sinks.

Experimental evidence

What we know about phloem transport has come from a number of experimental methods:

1. Analysis of phloem contents

Table 6.1 (below) shows what solutes are commonly found in the phloem of a number of species and in what relative amounts. Sucrose is by far the most abundant material present, comprising up to 80% of the total dry matter.

> **Key point**
> **Sucrose** is the form in which organic material is most commonly translocated in plants.

Inorganic ions are also present, sometimes in greater concentrations than in the xylem. It is not clear, however, whether the phloem can be described as a transport system for mineral ions. Because a solute is present in phloem sap it doesn't follow that it is there to be transported. Organic solutes are found in xylem sap but, by the same argument, the xylem is not generally regarded as a transport pathway for organic materials.

▶ Table 6.1: Solutes commonly occurring in phloem with their typical relative concentrations

Substance	Approximate concentration (mol m⁻³)
Sucrose	200 – 900
Amino acids	35 – 90
Organic acids (e.g. malic)	10 – 20
Mineral ions: e.g. K^+	40 - 100
Na^+	0.05 – 5.0
Cl^-	1 – 20
SO_4^-	0.3 – 1.0
NO_3^-	Nil

2. Aphid experiments

Phloem exudate can be obtained either by cutting into the phloem and collecting the sap that exudes from the cut, or by means of the **aphid stylet** technique. This involves cutting through the sucking mouthparts of a feeding aphid so that, in effect, a miniature hypodermic needle (the stylet of the insect) is left inserted in the plant, giving access to the contents of the phloem. It can be shown by microscopy that the aphid pushes its stylet into the space inside a single phloem sieve tube cell (see fig. 6.1).

Because the contents of the phloem are under pressure sap from inside the phloem will exude from a cut aphid stylet. The originators of the aphid stylet method, J. S. Kennedy and T. E. Mittler found that sap would exude from a cut stylet for several days at a rate of about 1mm³ per hour, allowing enough phloem sap to be collected for analysis. The continuing exudation proves that sap is constantly flowing through the phloem, because the total amount that can be collected from a single aphid stylet far exceeds the contents of a single phloem cell. It is also evidence that the contents of the phloem must be under pressure.

3. Using radioactive isotopes

When a radioactive form of carbon, either C^{14} or, in some cases, C^{11}, is introduced into organic molecules of a plant, either directly, as a component of the molecules themselves, or indirectly as carbon dioxide for photosynthesis, the movement and location of organic solutes can be traced. Autoradiographs of the whole plant or of transverse sections of the stem, made sometime after the introduction of the labelled carbon, show that:

- there is movement of labelled organic solutes away from their source
- the movement can be in either direction in the stem or root or in both directions simultaneously
- the labelled organic solutes are confined to the inside of phloem sieve tubes.

Key point
Translocation of organic solutes occurs in phloem sieve tubes.

4. The effect of girdling

The phloem can be removed from a living woody plant stem by stripping a complete ring of bark away from the wood. Alternatively the phloem surrounding a section of the stem can be killed by heat. Both treatments are referred to as **girdling** and effectively arrest phloem transport without interfering with transport in the xylem (wood). A girdled plant does not wilt and the parts above the girdle may even continue to grow. Eventually, however, the plant will die. Organic solutes cannot pass the girdled region. Consequently they accumulate on the side of the girdle nearest their source.

Key point
Girdling experiments, especially when used in conjunction with radioactive tracers, lead to the following conclusions:
- transport up the plant of water and mineral salts continues in the absence of phloem tissue and is therefore, in the xylem

- the transport of organic solutes occurs in the phloem because heat treatment renders the phloem ineffective in transporting organic solutes,
- living cells, or, at the very least, undamaged cells, must be required for phloem transport.

5. Phloem structure

Sieve tubes

Sieve tubes are made up of individual sieve cells or **sieve members** joined end to end in the same way that xylem cells join up to make xylem vessels. The similarity in structure between xylem vessels and phloem sieve tubes immediately suggests a transport role for both.

Sieve tubes are not completely open but are partially closed at intervals by cross walls called **sieve plates**. Sieve plates are full of holes through which the contents of the sieve tubes can pass. Despite the holes, sieve plates present a considerable resistance to the flow of solutes in the phloem.

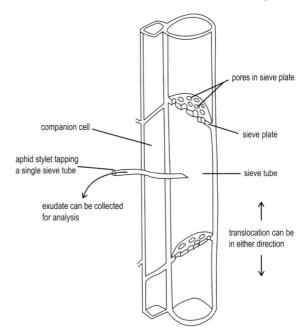

Fig. 6.1: Phloem structure

Companion cells

Each sieve element is associated with a cell called a companion cell. Quite what the function of the companion cells might be is not clear but their dense cytosol and numerous mitochondria suggest a metabolic role and their close association with sieve tubes suggests that their function is in maintaining phloem transport.

Loading and unloading of the phloem

The sucrose concentration inside the phloem sieve tubes of the minor veins of a leaf is generally two or three times as high as in the surrounding mesophyll cells. This suggests that sucrose is actively pumped into the sieve tubes against the concentration gradient, a phenomenon known as **phloem loading**.

Phloem loading requires metabolic energy. Movement against a concentration gradient is one indicator of this. Another is the fact that loading is selective. For example, sucrose may be loaded into the phloem while glucose and fructose are not. Some preferred amino acids are loaded; others not.

Unloading is the reverse of loading and occurs at the sinks. Sucrose and other solutes are actively removed from the phloem and passed to surrounding cells for metabolic activity or storage.

To a large extent the regulation of transport in the phloem is due to sink demand. When, for example, the developing tubers are removed from a potato plant (i.e. the sinks are removed) the amount of photosynthesis is reduced and the amount of sucrose travelling in the phloem is reduced accordingly. Wherever and whenever solutes are unloaded from the phloem a sink is created and sap flows in that direction. This explains why the direction of movement in the phloem can change and why it can be in two directions simultaneously.

The mechanism of phloem transport

Key point
The generally accepted explanation for the movement of solutes in the phloem is the **pressure flow** hypothesis.

The idea was first put forward by E. Munch in 1926. Essentially it involves a **mass flow** or **bulk flow** of the contents of phloem sieve tubes, pushed along by a pressure difference. The pressure difference originates osmotically and is due to the fact, firstly, that solutes are in higher concentration in the phloem where loading is taking place (the source) than in the surrounding tissues and, secondly, that solutes are constantly being removed from the phloem at the sink (fig. 6.2).

> **Key point**
> The movement of solutes in the phloem, according to the pressure flow theory, is a **passive** process but would not work without the **active** loading and unloading of solutes.

Evidence supporting the pressure flow mechanism

- the contents of the phloem **are** under pressure (see aphid stylet technique)
- there is a measurable osmotic potential difference between phloem sieve tubes and surrounding leaf cells at photosynthetic sources (e.g. around – 1.5 MPa for leaf cells and – 2.5 MPa for phloem sieve tubes)

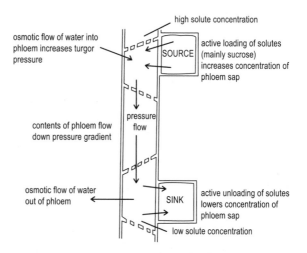

Fig. 6.2: Pressure flow mechanism of phloem transport

- phloem exudate collected near a source has a lower osmotic potential (higher solute concentration) than exudate collected near a sink
- there is usually a high concentration of solutes in the apoplast surrounding phloem sieve tubes in sink regions, favouring the osmotic movement of water out of sieve tubes
- observed rates of flow in the phloem (maximum velocities are of the order of 50 to 150 cm h^{-1}) can be accounted for by the calculated pressure drop between source and sink
- the holes in sieve plates are not blocked by protein as was once thought but are open to the free movement of the contents of one sieve tube cell into the next
- significant amounts of energy are not required for movement *per se* (as opposed to loading and unloading)

Remaining uncertainties

Although the pressure flow theory of phloem transport has almost reached the same level of acceptance as the cohesion theory of water movement in the xylem, there are still some questions, which need to be answered.

- If movement in the phloem is passive, why are the phloem sieve tubes not dead tissue, like the xylem?
- Does steam girdling have the same effect on translocation of organic solutes as complete removal of phloem tissue because heat denatures the proteins in sieve tubes and causes the sieve plates and tubes to be blocked or is it due to inhibition of metabolism?
- What is the function of the companion cells?
- Since the sieve plates offer considerable resistance to flow in the sieve tubes, why are they there?
- Can there be bi-directional movement within a single sieve tube? Claims for such bi-directional movement have been made, based on the results of experiments using radioactive tracers and the aphid stylet technique, but have been explained away, thereby leaving the mass flow concept intact. Clearly, the possibility of simultaneous flow in opposite directions in a single sieve tube is incompatible with a mass flow mechanism and it still cannot be categorically dismissed.

Tutorial

Progress questions

1. What evidence is there that the main route for the transport of organic solutes in a plant is the phloem?
2. What is meant by:
   i) source
   ii) sink
   iii) loading
   iv) unloading?
3. List some differences and similarities between xylem and phloem.

Seminar discussion

1. Evaluate the pressure flow hypothesis as an explanation of phloem transport.
2. Do any of the questions on p. 79 pose a serious threat to the pressure flow theory?

7 **Plant Movements**

One-minute overview

One way in which plants respond to internal and external stimuli is by movement of their parts. Movement is caused by differential elongation of the two sides of an organ, leading to bending. Elongation of cells during bending movements is either by growth or by uptake of water. Plant movements are adaptive and often have an obvious relationship with an environmental stimulus and a clear beneficial consequence.

In this chapter you will learn about:
- the nature of plant movements
- nomenclature and classification of plant movements
- nutations, nastic movements, tropisms and explosive mechanisms
- the perception of light, gravity, touch and other stimuli
- possible controlling mechanisms for plant responses.

The nature of plant movements

Like animals, plants move, or, at least, their parts move, but, in most cases, they do so only slowly. Movement in plants is brought about either by growth or by changes in the turgor of cells, neither of which can have effects as rapid as those brought about by the contractile fibres of animal cells. Plants do not generally have a rapid communication system equivalent to the nervous system of many animal types.

The common mechanism of movements

Plant movements are brought about by a differential expansion of cells on two opposing sides of an organ. The cells on one side expand faster than those on the other. The increase in size of cells may be due to the absorption of water (turgor change) or to growth. Turgor changes are reversible but growth is irreversible. When the two sides of an organ, such as a stem or root or leaf petiole expand at different rates the result, inevitably, is bending. The same principle is seen in a bimetallic strip used in a thermostat. Because the two metals that make up the strip have different rates of thermal expansion the strip bends towards the slower expanding side as the temperature rises.

> **Key point**
> Plant movements are caused by the bending of plant organs.

The need for responsiveness

Movement and responses to stimuli are essential adaptive features of plants. It is vital, for example, that, as a seed germinates the root grows downward towards a source of water and the shoot grows upwards towards the light. Flowers have to open if insects are to have access for pollination but it is a good idea for them to close in cold, wet weather and at night. Climbing plants can only attach themselves to a support because organs such as tendrils are sensitive to touch and respond by clinging on. Photosynthesis is most effective when leaves are moved to positions where they can best intercept the available light.

> **Key point**
> Plant movements are adaptive, bringing about some obvious benefit for the survival of the plant.

Types of plant movements

Plant movements are classified according to:
- whether they are growth or turgor movements
- whether or not they are a response to an external stimulus
- the type of stimulus
- whether or not the stimulus is a directional one

- the direction of the response and the relationship (if there is one) between it and the direction of the stimulus.

> **Key point**
> There are three classes of plant movement:
> - Nutations
> - Nastic movements
> - Tropisms or tropic movements

Nutations

These are the circular growth movements of, most typically, stems as they increase in height. The tip of the stem follows a helical path as if it is feeling its way upwards. There is no apparent environmental stimulus for nutations, nor any clear advantage for the plant, except in the case of climbing plants, where the movement of the shoot in a circular path increases its chances of making contact with a suitable support.

Nastic movements

> **Key point**
> Nastic movements are responses to **non-directional** stimuli. Although the response itself may be directional (sleep movements of leaves, for example, where the leaf stalk bends upwards and downwards alternately) the stimulus has no direction to it.

Examples of nastic movements are the raising and lowering of leaves, the closing and opening of flowers and the operation of the Venus fly trap. They may be the result of growth or, in other cases, turgor changes. Some nastic movements are the obvious and direct result of a stimulus (e.g. a fly landing on a fly trap) while some may be related to an environmental signal but also linked to the plant's natural rhythm (e.g. sleep movements of leaves), in which case they can continue even when the stimulus is missing. The sleep movements of the leaves of some species, for example, go on for several cycles in constant darkness.

Tropisms

> **Key point**
> A tropism is a **directional growth** response to a **directional** stimulus

The direction of the response may be related to the direction of the stimulus in various ways. For example a root that has been displaced from its natural position will often grow downwards in response to gravity whereas a shoot will tend to grow in exactly the opposite direction. The root is growing in the same direction as the stimulus (gravity is a force acting downwards) while the shoot is growing at 180° to it. Some plant organs, stolons, for example grow at a 90° angle to gravity (i.e. horizontally).

Nomenclature

Different types of plant movement are given definitive names that indicate whether they are nastic or tropic movements, the nature of the stimulus involved and, in the case of tropisms in which direction the response occurs relative to the direction of the stimulus. So, for example, **positive phototropism** is a **tropism** that involves growth of an organ **towards** a source of **light**; **negative gravitropism** is growth in the **opposite** direction to the force of **gravity**. The table below summarises the various types of plant movement with examples in each case.

Type of movement	Description	Examples
Nastic movements	(Greek *nastos* means 'pressed close')	
epinasty	general term for downward bending	leaf stalks
hyponasty	upward bending	leaf stalks
nyctinasty	sleep movements (Greek *nux* = night)	leaf hyponasty at night

Continued

Type of movement	Description	Examples
thermonasty	opening and closing according to temperature	flower petals close in cold weather, open in warm
hydronasty (hygronasty)	response to water stress caused by differential turgor changes	some leaves roll up in dry conditions
thigmonasty	response to touch (Gr. *thigma = touch*)	Mimosa - the sensitive plant – leaves close when touched
Tropisms	(Gr. *trope* = 'turn')	
phototropism	response to a light gradient	
positive phototropism	bending towards the light	shoots and coleoptiles
negative phototropism	bending away from light	the young shoots of some climbing plants grow towards darkness
dia-phototropism	growing at 90° to light intensity gradient	'solar tracking' by leaves
gravitropism	response to gravity (also called **geotropism**)	
positive gravitropism	bending downwards	roots, especially seedling roots
negative gravitropism	bending upwards	shoots and coleoptiles
dia-gravitropism	growing horizontally	stolons and rhizomes
plagio-gravitropism	growing at an angle to the vertical but not a strict 90°	side shoots and side roots
thigmotropism	bending in response to touch	tendrils and climbing stems
hydrotropism (hygrotropism)	response to a water potential gradient (towards higher W.P.)	some roots

Three steps to movement

Key point

A plant movement is a three step process:
 i) **Perception** (of the stimulus)
 ii) **Transduction** (of a signal to the site of the response)
 iii) **Response** (cellular changes that cause the observed movement)

Of these three stages the second is the least understood. In fact it would be fair to say that understanding of the link between stimulus detection and the growth or turgor changes in cells that bring about plant movements is very limited in all cases. For this reason we shall leave consideration of this stage till last.

Perception of stimuli

Light

The most effective wavelengths of light for phototropism are in the blue and ultra violet parts of the spectrum. The photoreceptor molecule or molecules, therefore, should show peak absorption of these wavelengths. The most likely candidates are the yellow pigments, **carotenoids** and **flavoproteins**. Evidence presently favours a flavoprotein but the involvement of other pigments cannot be ruled out. Because the identity of the pigment (or pigments) initiating phototropism is unknown, it is referred to as **cryptochrome**.

Two points to bear in mind about the perception of light in phototropism are:

i) certain regions of a plant organ are more sensitive to light than others and these parts are not necessarily the regions where the response is centred (see section on transduction); Darwin's original experiments on phototropism showed that the tip of a coleoptile was most sensitive to light but the bending response occurred in all regions (see Ch. 8).

ii) what is perceived is a **gradient** of light intensity, not necessarily a total contrast of light and dark.

Gravity

The way in which plants detect the direction of the force of gravity is by means of specialised cells called **statocytes.** In the statocytes there are plastids, usually laden with starch, (therefore **amyloplasts**) that sediment within the cell in response to gravity (fig. 7.1). Sedimenting bodies of this type are referred to as **statoliths**.

A body of evidence supports the role of statocytes and statoliths in the perception of gravity in gravitropism:

- practically all plant organs that respond to gravity contain starch statoliths; this is even true of some species that do not normally manufacture starch
- statoliths can be observed to sediment in statocytes to the lowermost side of the cell
- the rate of sedimentation correlates well with the **presentation time** for a tissue (the minimum time that a plant organ needs to be displaced from its previous position in order to achieve a gravitropic response)
- when a plant is treated in such a way that all the starch in statocytes is removed it becomes insensitive to gravity
- sensitivity to gravity appears, or reappears in plants from which all starch has been removed, only after new starch grains are formed in plastids
- mutants of maize with very small amyloplasts are relatively insensitive to gravity.
- a mechanical force such as that generated by a centrifuge can move statoliths inside cells and also cause growth rate changes

As with phototropism, in gravitropism the site of detection of the stimulus is not necessarily the same as the site of the response. Statocytes are confined, for example, to the root cap in roots but it is the region behind the root cap that bends in response to a displacement of the root from vertical. In the absence of a root cap, a root will no longer respond to a change in position with respect to gravity – further evidence for the gravity detecting role of amyloplasts.

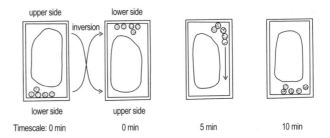

Fig. 7.1: Sedimentation of amyloplasts in a statocyte
At time 0 min the structure (e.g. a stem) in which the statocyte was located was turned upside down, leading to the sedimentation of the amyloplasts to the opposite end of the cell. The timescale given is typical for sedimentation in gravisensitive cells.

Touch

Plants are sensitive to touch and touch initiates not only nastic responses and tropic responses but also morphogenetic responses (rubbing or brushing plants often makes them grow shorter and stockier). Very little is known, however, about how touch (or pressure) is detected; for example, whether certain cells alone are sensitive and whether only certain parts of cells.

Other stimuli

The detection phase of responses to water potential gradients, temperature changes, mechanical stress and other stimuli has been relatively little researched. In many cases the stimulus may have a direct effect rather than give rise to a signal (e.g. loss of water from cells to a dry atmosphere, causing turgor change).

Responses

i) Nastic movements

Nastic movements are generally faster than tropisms. Often the bending that gives rise to the movements occurs in specialised areas. Many leaves, for example, have, at the base of their petiole, a thickened region known as a **pulvinus**. Movements of the leaf are brought about by differential expansion of cells on opposite sides of the pulvinus.

Many nastic movements are caused by the swelling of cells due to the rapid uptake of water (turgor changes). The mechanism involved is similar to that causing opening of stomata. Potassium ions are redistributed, pumped into some cells and out of others, and water follows passively by osmosis. When cells on one side of an organ such as a leaf pulvinus lose water and those on the other side become more turgid, then the organ bends (see fig. 7.2).

Other nastic movements are produced by differential growth. For example leaves that have no pulvini at their base can still show epinasty by means of the upper side of the leaf petiole growing faster than the underside, and hyponasty when the reverse happens.

ii) Tropisms

Whenever a plant organ develops a tropic curvature it is because one side has grown more than the other (see fig. 7.3). It does not follow that growth on one side must have been accelerated and growth on the other slowed down. If growth rate of both sides were reduced but of one side more than the other, that would have the same effect. There are several possibilities for growth rate changes responsible for tropic bending. What actually happens to growth rates during tropism is obviously important to an understanding of how the process is controlled and it is surprising, therefore, that detailed information about such changes has only been gathered relatively recently.

Signal transduction

Often the site of perception of a stimulus that brings about a plant movement is not where the movement itself is effected. There is a need, therefore, for a form of communication between cells. This is what is referred to as **signal transduction**.

Even if the cell that responds to a stimulus is the same cell that detected the stimulus, there is still a need for conversion of the signal into a response. For example the sedimentation of statoliths in a cell in response to a change in the gravity vector

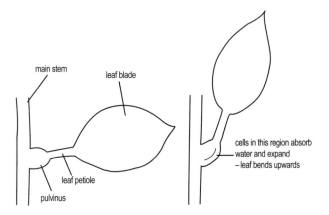

Fig. 7.2: An example of a nastic movement (leaf hyponasty)

cannot, by itself, cause any growth change in that or any other cell. Nor can the action of light on a pigment alone have any effect on growth. There must be a chain of events connecting stimulus detection and growth rate or turgor change.

> **Key point**
> Signal transduction is the area about which there is greatest uncertainty in the field of plant responses.

The involvement of plant hormones

The concept of plant hormones started with the study of phototropism in grass coleoptiles (see Ch. 8). Differential growth during phototropic bending was explained by the uneven distribution of a growth accelerating hormone across the plant organ that was doing the bending. The hormone was called **auxin**.

Auxin

The relationship between auxin and plant movements can be summed up as follows:

- auxin, as a controller of cell elongation, is almost certainly involved in some tropic movements
- there is little evidence for the involvement of auxin in nastic movements

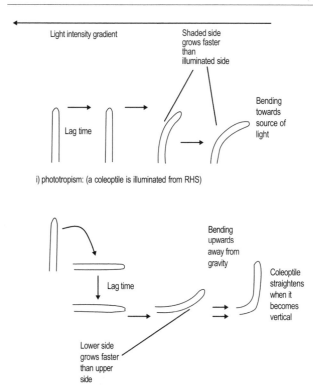

i) phototropism: (a coleoptile is illuminated from RHS)

ii) gravitropism: a coleoptile is placed on its side

Fig. 7.3: The events of phototropism and gravitropism in cereal coleoptiles
Lag time refers to a period of usually about twenty minites during which no change can be absorbed.

- auxin applied externally to one side of a plant organ can produce bending that mimics tropic bending
- stimulation of some plant organs by, for example, lighting from one side or displacement from an upright to a horizontal position, can affect the concentrations of auxin within the tissue and create auxin concentration gradients in the predicted direction across the organ
- conflicting evidence as to the role of auxin in tropisms comes from experiments on different organs and different types of tropism
- much remains unresolved, especially the mechanism by which auxin might be redistributed or synthesised within tissues as a result of a tropic stimulus

- what may be more important than the auxin **content** of tissues is the **sensitivity** to auxin of different cells and this is the factor that may be altered whenever an organ is stimulated prior to a tropic response.

Inhibitors

Inhibition of growth on one side of a plant organ will have the same bending effect as acceleration of the growth rate of the opposite side. Inhibitors have been implicated in shoot phototropism and, in particular, root gravitropism. Ironically the inhibitor in roots may well be auxin. Auxin is inhibitory to root cell elongation at concentrations that promote shoot growth.

Turgorin

The turgor changes that occur in some leaf pulvinus cells and cause epinasty or hyponasty of the leaves, can be induced by, as yet, unidentified chemical substances. In *Mimosa*, for example, when one leaf is touched a substance is caused to move through the xylem to other leaves. Several leaves, not just the one that was touched, then fold up in the typical thigmonastic response of this 'sensitive' plant. Diffusible chemicals that bring about turgor changes in leaf pulvini are called **turgorins**.

Electrical phenomena

A few plant movements are quite fast. Two that have been studied extensively are the thigmonastic response of *Mimosa* - the leaves of this plant close within seconds of being touched or shaken – and the rapid closing of the Venus' fly trap. In both cases signal transduction is by means of an electrical action potential caused by the rapid pumping of ions across cell membranes and set off by the initial stimulus. In Mimosa the action potential travels at up to 2 cm s^{-1}, fast for a plant but still much slower than nervous conduction.

Calcium

Movement of calcium ions accompanies gravitropic bending of roots. Calcium ions move towards the lower side of a horizontally placed root and application of calcium to one side of a root causes bending towards that side. Quite how the involvement of calcium fits into the whole picture of the control of root gravitropism, however, is not clear.

Explosive mechanisms

Explosive mechanisms, such as the catapulting of seeds out of a ripe seed pod fall into none of the three categories mentioned earlier. The movement itself does not involve growth or any change in cell size but is a sudden release of tension, like the bursting of a balloon when it is over-inflated. Some fruits, like those of the Himalayan balsam (*Impatiens glandulifera*) explode as turgor builds up in the cells, while others, like gorse (*Ulex europaeus*), break open forcefully as they dry.

In cases like these there is no control mechanism to be determined. The response is an inevitable result of a combination of the design of the fruit and the swelling or shrinking of cells during its development.

Tutorial

Progress questions

1. Plant movements are adaptive. Give some examples.
2. Define and distinguish beween: nutations, nastic movements and tropisms.
3. In which direction will a plant organ grow if it is:
    i) negatively gravitropic,
    ii) positively gravitropic,
    iii) diagravitropic?
4. Why are plant movements usually slow?

Seminar discussion

1. At one time all tropisms could be neatly accounted for by means of the 'Cholodney – Went' theory, which relied entirely for its explanation on the growth controlling influence of auxin. To what extent has more recent evidence put paid to this theory? And what remains?

Practical assignments

1. It is easy to observe plant movements for yourself. Try displacing any shoot organ from vertical to horizontal and watching what happens over the next few hours. Or grow seedlings in a box with a window on only one side to observe phototropism. See if you can measure the presentation time and the lag time for a tropic response.

> **Study tip**
> 1. Keep an open mind in your reading about this topic. Remember that the control of plant movements is still very poorly understood.

8   Plant Growth Substances

One-minute overview

Plants synthesise chemical substances that act as controllers of growth, development and other physiological events. They are effective in very small concentrations, can move around the plant from places where they are made, to places where they exert their influence and are called plant growth substances or plant hormones. There are five recognised groups of plant growth substance and others that have yet to reach quite the same status.

In this chapter you will learn about:
- the plant growth substance concept
- the main types of plant growth substance
- their synthesis, metabolism, activity, transport and characteristic effects
- how plant growth substances work

What are plant growth substances?

Key point
A **plant growth substance** is an organic compound that is produced in plant tissues and, in very small amounts, has profound effects on growth, development or other physiological events within the plant.

Often a plant growth substance is synthesised in one part of a plant and is transported to a quite separate part, where it exerts its effect. For this reason, drawing a direct comparison with the hormones of animals, plant growth substances are also called **plant hormones**.

What are not plant growth substances?

Mineral salts, even though they have profound effects on plants, are not plant growth substances because they are not organic and are not synthesised by the plant. Organic compounds such as sugars and amino acids are not plant growth substances because they have no effects at the very low concentrations at which plant growth substances are active (down to 1μM, or less in some cases). Other naturally occurring compounds, pigments, for example, cannot be described as plant growth substances because they are not mobile within the plant.

Chemical nature

- all plant growth substances are relatively small molecules, the largest having a skeleton of about twenty carbon atoms
- the smallest of all is ethene (ethylene), C_2H_4
- although plant growth substances may be chemically related to other types of molecule found within cells, they do not belong to any of the more familiar biochemical groups, such as carbohydrates, amino acids, fatty acids or proteins.

The discovery of auxin

Auxin was the first plant growth substance to be recognised. The story of its discovery (see fig. 8.1) embraces many of the ideas and criteria that define the plant growth substance concept, namely:

- the need in plants for communication between parts
- the idea of a transmissible chemical message
- a site of synthesis and a site of action
- effectiveness of very low concentrations of the chemical signal
- an effect on the growth or development of target cells or tissues
- a controlling function for an adaptive response (in this case phototropism)
- related effects of an endogenous plant growth substance (one that is synthesised and acts within the tissues of the

plant) and exogenous (exogenous means 'added to the outside') applications of the same substance.

Classes of plant growth substance

Key point
There are five recognised groups of plant growth substance:
- **Auxins**
- **Gibberellins**
- **Cytokinins**
- **Ethene (ethylene)**
- **Inhibitors (abscisic acid)**

In addition there are a number of hypothetical or partially determined growth substances that may, in time, reach the same state of recognition as the five listed, e.g. turgorin.

What defines a group?

With the exception of ethene, the types of plant growth substances have plural names. In other words there are more than one auxin, more than one gibberellin, more than one cytokinin and more than one inhibitor (though often the inhibitor, abscisic acid, is considered separately from other inhibitors and forms a group by itself).

Key point
Each group of plant growth substances is defined by the characteristic effects the members of the group have on plant growth.

So, all auxins have similar effects on plant growth and development and their effects are quite distinct from those of, for example, gibberellins.

Auxins

- promote the elongation of stem tissue at concentrations up to about 10^{-5} M

i) Darwin's experiments (1881) coleoptiles illuminated from the right hand side

Darwin's experiments showed that the tip of a coleoptile perceives the light stimulus but the tropic response occurs in regions below the tip, thus suggesting the need for a form of communication.

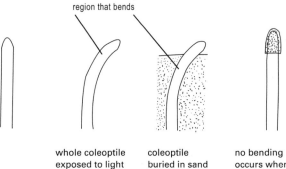

region that bends

| whole coleoptile exposed to light bends towards light | coleoptile buried in sand still bends as long as the tip is exposed | no bending occurs when the tip is covered by an opaque cap |

ii) Went's experiments (1928)

Went's experiments demonstrated the production by coleoptile tips of a diffusible growth promoting substance. This substance was called auxin.

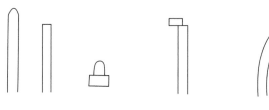

| tip of coleoptile cut off and placed on gelatin | diffusible substance (auxin) collected in gelatin block | when gelatin block containing auxin is put on one side of a decapitated coleoptile the coleoptile bends |

Fig. 8.1: The discovery of auxin – experiments with grass and cereal coleoptiles

- inhibit the growth of roots at concentrations above about 10^{-8} M
- stimulate the initiation of roots on cuttings
- control apical dominance (see Ch. 10)
- delay the abscission of leaves.

Gibberellins

- increase stem elongation in genetically dwarf plants
- promote the 'bolting' and premature flowering of rosette plants
- bring about seed germination by switching on enzyme systems and overcoming light or cold requirement.

Cytokinins

- stimulate cell division
- act with auxins to determine the pattern of differentiation of cells
- delay senescence and mobilise nutrients in plant tissues
- overcome the correlative inhibition of axillary buds (see Ch. 10).

Ethene

- promotes fruit ripening
- causes the 'triple response' of seedlings: reduction in growth, thickening and loss of gravitropic response
- normally suppresses flowering but can promote it in some species
- can promote seed germination.

Inhibitors

- as the name suggests, inhibit growth of many plant organs
- cause dormancy of e.g. seeds and buds
- abscisic acid regulates stomatal closing in water stressed plants
- abscisic acid is an antagonist of gibberellins in enzyme induction in germinating seeds.

The effects included above are **typical**. In other words they define the substance and, therefore, any chemical having these effects must belong to the relevant group. Consequently members of the groups include both naturally occurring and synthetic substances. For example, the compound **indoleacetic acid (IAA)** is a naturally occurring auxin while **2,4 dichlorophenoxyacetic acid (2,4D)** is also classed as an auxin even though it is a synthetic growth regulator, used as a weedkiller.

Exogenous and endogenous action

Are the effects listed above just responses that are brought about by exogenous application of the various growth substances or are they processes that are controlled endogenously by those same growth substances? The answer, in most cases is both. A lot of evidence for the role of growth substances has come from observing the effects of their external application; but this evidence, by itself, is not enough to implicate growth substances in the control of processes occurring naturally. Only when additional evidence is accumulated, such as measurements of the concentrations of a growth substance in plant tissues and changes in those concentrations during growth and development, can the full picture become clearer.

Other defining criteria

To some extent the members of each group of growth substances are also chemically related (see fig. 8.2).

The site of production and transport characteristics of a growth substance may also be a feature of the group to which it belongs; e.g. synthesis of auxins is associated with young growing tissues such as shoot apices and developing leaves; auxin transport tends to be from the top to the base of shoots. Cytokinins, on the other hand, are often produced in the roots and move upwards in the xylem.

The specific cells and tissues (the so called target cells) that react to a particular plant growth substance and the specific mode of action of the different growth substances are also characteristic.

Notes on the five groups of growth substances

1. Auxins

- *Types:* There are at least four naturally occurring substances with auxin activity. They are: **indoleacetic acid (IAA)**, **4-chloroindoleacetic acid**, **phenylacetic acid** and **indolebutyric acid**. Of these the first, IAA, is the best known and was for a long time thought to be the only naturally

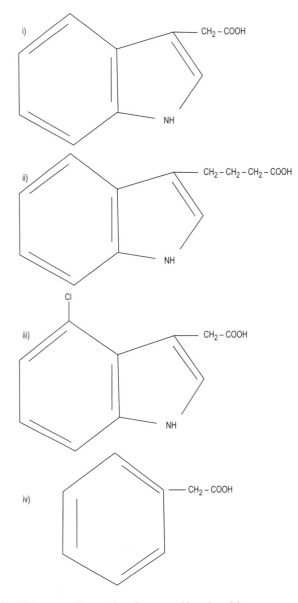

Fig. 8.2: Four naturally occurring substances with auxin activity

i)   indoleacetic acid (IAA)

ii) indolebutyric acid

iii) chloroindoleacetic acid

iv) phenylacetic acid

occurring auxin. Other similar molecules found in plants are probably auxin precursors.

- *Synthesis*: Auxins are similar in structure to the amino acid tryptophan and are believed to be synthesised from this compound. Synthesis usually takes place in young growing tissues.

- *Metabolism:* Auxin levels in tissues are controlled by: i) synthesis ii) binding to other molecules and iii) break down. Bound auxin is inactive but can be transported and acts as an auxin store. Breakdown of auxin is by means of oxidase enzymes such as **IAA oxidase**.

- *Transport:* Auxin transport is rarely through either the phloem or the xylem but predominantly in parenchyma cells. Movement is characteristically polar, from top to base in stems and leaf petioles and in the opposite direction in roots. The rate of movement is about 1 cm h^{-1} and the polarity of movement is unaffected by the position of an organ with respect to gravity. Polar auxin movement is an active, energy requiring process, faster than could be accounted for by diffusion alone.

- *Activity:* Different tissues show remarkably different sensitivities to applied auxin. Extension growth in stem sections, for example, is promoted by external concentrations of IAA between 10^{-8} and 10^{-5}M, whereas concentrations above as little as 10^{-8} M are inhibitory to root growth.

2. Gibberellins

- *Types:* Over 70 types of gibberellin have been identified in higher plants. All are chemically very similar, consisting of a skeleton of either 19 or 20 carbon atoms arranged in a four or five ring structure. The different types are identified by a number, GA_1, GA_2, GA_3, etc., GA standing for gibberellic acid. Not all types have exactly the same effects but there is enough correspondence between the activity of the different types to group them together. GA_3 is the most commonly available gibberellin and is the one usually referred to when the name **gibberellic acid** is used.

- *Synthesis:* Probably most living plant cells synthesise gibberellins. Known sources of gibberellins are roots, young leaves and seeds.
- *Metabolism:* Most gibberellins seem to be rapidly metabolised to inactive products in growing tissues.
- *Transport:* Movement of gibberellins is not polar like that of auxin and occurs mainly in the phloem and xylem.
- *Activity:* The effect of gibberellins on stem elongation (see p. 99) is unique. It is most noticeable in genetically dwarf plants and in biennial rosette plants prior to flowering and involves an effect on cell division as well as cell elongation.

3. Cytokinins

- *Types:* There are believed to be a number of naturally occurring cytokinins. Several other related compounds not produced in plant tissues are also highly active in bringing about the same physiological responses. All these compounds are chemically related to the purine, **adenine**, one of the component bases of DNA and RNA. Indeed, **kinetin**, the first cytokinin to be identified, was a breakdown product of herring sperm DNA. The chemical relationship to adenine is often used as a defining feature of a cytokinin.
- *Synthesis:* Cytokinins are probably synthesised in young tissues and in root tips, though the evidence is not conclusive. The strongest evidence is for synthesis in root tips.
- *Metabolism:* Cytokinins can be inactivated by oxidase enzymes or by conjugation with other molecules, such as glucose.
- *Transport:* Cytokinins are known to be transported from root to shoot in the xylem. Phloem sieve tubes also contain cytokinins: there may, therefore, be some transport in the phloem. Cytokinins applied to the surfaces of leaves rarely move far from the point of application. This and other evidence suggests that, apart from upward movement in the transpiration stream, transport of cytokinins in the plant is limited.

- *Activity:* The role of cytokinins in activating cell division in plant tissue cultures not only led to the discovery of kinetin by Carlos Miller in 1954, but has also become the definitive test for a cytokinin. Of all the known actions of cytokinins, their ability to initiate cell division is considered the most characteristic.

4. Inhibitors

- *Types:* There are a number of substances found in plants that have an inhibitory effect on growth, in addition to auxin and ethene, both of which can inhibit growth in certain circumstances. There seems to be no relationship between the various inhibitory substances and it is unclear whether some of them can be classed as true plant hormones. One such inhibitor, however, **abscisic acid (ABA)**, has been studied far more extensively than any other, to the point that its status as a plant growth substance alongside the other four groups is assured. Most texts put ABA in a group by itself and treat other inhibitors separately. This is for two reasons. Firstly so much more is known about ABA – it was the first such growth substance to be studied intensively – and, secondly, it is more than just an inhibitor of growth. ABA is known to be involved in the control of a number of adaptive responses in plants.
- *Synthesis:* ABA is a 15 carbon compound, synthesised by the breakdown of carotenoids, the pigments found in chloroplasts and other plastids.
- *Metabolism:* Inactivation of ABA can occur in two ways: i) attachment of a glucose molecule to form an inactive conjugate (as can happen with IAA, gibberellins and cytokinins), ii) aerobic oxidation.
- *Transport:* The movement of ABA in plants is much the same as that of gibberellins. It moves readily in both phloem and xylem. It is also transported, in a non-polar way, through parenchyma cells.
- *Activity:* ABA is sometimes referred to as a 'stress hormone'. When plants are stressed by, for example, drought, cold or high salinity, ABA levels in the tissues rise and bring

about protective responses, such as stomatal closure, leaf fall and frost 'hardening'. The stimulus for the synthesis of ABA is loss of cell turgor.

5. Ethene

- *Types:* Ethene (or ethylene as it used to be called) is doubly unique amongst plant growth substances in that, firstly, it shares its group with no other substance and, secondly, it is a gas at normal temperature and pressure. It is also an unusually small molecule for any biologically active compound, having a molecular weight of just 28.
- *Synthesis:* All parts of a plant produce ethene, though some parts are more productive than others. Roots, for example, generally produce less ethene than shoots. Synthesis is from the amino acid methionine and is an oxygen requiring conversion. So, anaerobic conditions inhibit ethene production. Several factors promote synthesis: wounding, mechanical stress (e.g. pressure), darkness, carbon dioxide and placing a stem horizontal, amongst them.
- *Metabolism and transport:* Ethene, being a gas, diffuses most readily through intercellular spaces. Movement through water is about ten thousand times slower than through air. The ability of ethene to diffuse through and out of plant tissues affects its concentration and the length of time it remains in the plant and, therefore, its biological effects. For example, although, when the soil in which a plant is growing becomes waterlogged, ethene production is inhibited by lack of oxygen, the reduced diffusion of the gas through water actually causes its concentration to rise. One of the effects of increased ethene concentration, in these circumstances, is degradation of root cell walls.
- *Activity:* Ethene action illustrates well the principle of target cells and different sensitivities to a growth substance of apparently similar cells. Ethene, for example, causes leaf epinasty by increasing the elongation of parenchyma cells on the upper side of the leaf petiole, without affecting the equivalent cells on the lower side. It is not clear why the response of the upper and lower cells is different any

more than the fact that ethene can increase elongation of some cells when, more usually, it inhibits growth. In stem tissues IAA can increase the production of ethene several hundred fold. Many responses to IAA have been attributed to this effect on ethene production. It appears, however, that ethene and IAA often have similar but independent effects (e.g. promotion of adventitious root formation on stem cuttings).

Other plant growth substances

In addition to the five groups of plant growth substances described above there are a number of other candidates for inclusion as plant hormones. In some cases insufficient is known about their characteristics and activity to raise them to the same status as the better known growth substances; or there is doubt about them satisfying all the criteria defining a plant hormone. There may, for example, be little evidence of their mobility in plant tissues. Lastly, in some cases, the evidence for a hormone may be very strong but the identity of the substance itself remains a mystery. For example:

Salicylic acid

Salicylic acid is the active ingredient in aspirin. One of its more unusual effects as a plant hormone is to cause an increase in the rate of respiration and thereby produce heat in some flowers. This, in turn, helps to evaporate the volatile molecules that attract insects.

Florigen (flowering hormone)

There is abundant evidence that, in many species, a hormone is involved in the initiation of flowering. When, for example, a single leaf of a plant that normally flowers in response to a certain length of daylight is given the required daylength stimulus, the plant will flower, despite the rest of it being kept in constant light. Some message must travel from the leaf, where the inductive stimulus is detected, to the shoot apex, where the change from vegetative growth to floral development takes place. This and other observations clearly implicate a hormonal control mechanism for flowering. The problem is that no such hormone has ever been isolated and identified. It remains a hypothetical plant growth substance and is named **florigen**.

Turgorin

This is the 'touch hormone' of sensitive plants (see Ch. 7).

Jasmonic acid

Jasmonates are molecules produced as a result of wounding. They have two effects, one is to inhibit many active growth processes, the other to promote the formation of ethene. They speed up the senescence of leaves and although their function is uncertain a role in leaf senescence seems likely.

How do growth substances work?

At present, no one really knows. Parts of the story, however, can be told:

- the fact that plant growth substances are active in such minute amounts suggests that they must act only as signals or switches.
- the complex nature of some plant growth substance effects, involving a number of separate but related processes, is further evidence for their role as switches.
- proteins that bind specifically to plant hormones have been identified. These **receptor proteins** represent the first step in control by growth substances – the perception of the hormone by the target cells.
- there is considerable evidence that growth substances act at the gene level. Both new messenger RNA synthesis and protein synthesis can take place within minutes of application of a growth substance. Enzyme production has long been known to be a direct effect of some plant growth substances (e.g. amylase synthesis in germinating cereal grains as a result of gibberellin action).
- specific aspects of the mechanism of action of some plant growth substances are known. For example auxins promote cell elongation by 'loosening' cell walls

so that they stretch more easily under turgor pressure. Gibberellins promote cell growth by increasing the hydrolysis of complex carbohydrates into simple sugars. There are many more examples.

- the action of one growth substance may be through its effect on another. The promotion of ethene synthesis by auxin has already been mentioned. In Ch.10 you will read about how auxin from the apex of a plant can cause a build up of inhibitors in axillary buds.

- as a general principle plant growth substances often act together. A good example is in the differentiation of callus tissue in tissue culture experiments. Depending on the relative concentrations of auxin and cytokinin in the culture medium, the undifferentiated tissue will develop roots or shoots or both or simply grow but remain undifferentiated.

- the orchestration of the activity of growth substances depends on their levels being controlled within the plant. This is implemented by: i) synthesis, ii) retrieval of the hormone from an inactive form, iii) transport from another site, iv) inactivation or breakdown.

- hormone levels are often affected by environmental and internal stimuli. This allows for correlations between plant development and environmental conditions and between different parts of the plant. Ch.10 examines this feature of plant growth in more detail.

Key point
The way in which plant growth substances work is one of the most important as yet relatively little understood fields of plant physiology.

Tutorial

Progress questions

1. What is a plant growth substance?
2. Name the five main groups of plant growth substances.
3. What other plant growth substances are there?
4. What effects would you expect a solution of each of the following to have on aspects of plant growth:
   i) an auxin
   ii) a gibberellin
   iii) a cytokinin
   iv) abscisic acid ?
5. What is unusual about ethene as a plant growth substance?
6. How do plant growth substances work?

Seminar discussion

1. What types of evidence indicate that an aspect of a plant's natural growth or development is controlled by endogenous plant growth substances? Is one type of evidence (e.g. the effect of exogenous applications of a plant growth substance) enough by itself?

Practical assignments

Find out about the use of synthetic plant growth substances (plant growth regulators) in horticulture and agriculture.

9 Photomorpho-genesis, Phytochrome and Photoperiodism

One-minute overview

Very small doses of light can bring about major developmental changes in plants, described as photomorphogenetic changes; for example, germination and de-etiolation. The pigment that detects light in most examples of photomorphogenesis is phytochrome. Phytochrome exists in two interchangeable forms: Pr and Pfr. Pr absorbs red light and in doing so is converted to Pfr while Pfr absorbs far red light and is converted to Pr. The Pfr form is active in promoting photomorphogenetic events.

A number of aspects of plant development, such as flowering, are sensitive to the length of the day, a phenomenon known as photoperiodicity. Phytochrome detects the presence of light in photoperiodic responses but some other system, involving time measurement is also required to explain them.

In this chapter you will learn about:
- examples of photomorphogenesis
- the nature and properties of phytochrome
- high irradiance reactions and very low fluence responses
- the environmental significance of the phytochrome response
- photoperiodism and flowering

Light effects

Photosynthesis and phototropism are two ways in which plants react to light (Ch. 2 & 7). Light is also the stimulus for a distinct class of developmental responses known collectively as **photomorphogenetic** responses.

> **Key point**
> **Photomorphogenesis** is any irreversible change to the structural development, appearance or form of a plant initiated by a light stimulus.

Phototropism could be included under this heading but is usually not, because it only involves growth changes as opposed to developmental changes and relies on a different light detecting system to that involved in the majority of photomorphogenetic effects.

Both photomorphogenesis and phototropism rely on light only as a signal to kick-start a process. Light is not required for the continuation of the process itself. In photosynthesis light is used continuously and quantitatively. Up to a point the more light a plant absorbs the more it photosynthesises. The amounts of light needed to produce a photomorphogenetic effect, however, can be very small indeed and additional light does not always make the response any greater.

Examples of photomorphogenesis

- reduction of elongation of stem growth in **etiolated** seedlings
- leaf and cotyledon expansion
- plumular hook opening or hypocotyl hook opening
- chloroplast development and chlorophyll synthesis
- synthesis of the purple pigments, **anthocyanins**
- seed germination
- more rarely, inhibition of seed germination
- flowering or prevention of flowering in photoperiodically sensitive plants

Light responses of etiolated seedlings

The first four responses in the list above are collectively referred to as **de-etiolation**, i.e. the reversal of **etiolation**. When a seed germinates in darkness the shoot becomes **etiolated** and has the characteristics shown in fig. 9.1.

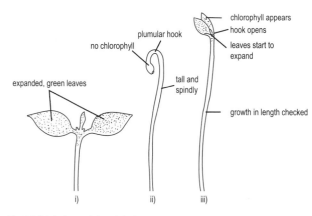

Fig. 9.1: Etiolation and de-etiolation

   i) light grown seedling

  ii) dark grown, etiolated seedling

iii) dark grown seedling placed in the light (de-etiolated)

As soon as an etiolated shoot reaches the light its character changes. This is a classic case of photomorphogenesis (fig. 9.1).

It is not hard to see the advantage of etiolation to a green plant. Growth in height is maximised while effort put into developing photosynthesising systems is conserved until light is available. The shoot can afford to grow spindly because it is likely to be supported by soil or sheltered by whatever cover is excluding the light. The plumular or hypocotyl hook protects the shoot tip as it is carried upward through the soil.

Once in the light the imperative for the plant is to develop its photosynthesising apparatus as quickly as possible and to support it effectively - not to grow in height at all costs.

Action spectrum for photomorphogenesis

What wavelengths of light are most effective in bringing about photomorphogenetic responses? They are wavelengths in the red region of the light spectrum and the same for almost all photomorphogenetic responses that have been studied. Wavelengths of between about 600 and 680 nm are most effective in promoting, for example, the germination of seeds, the opening of the hooked tips of seedling shoots and leaf expansion in etiolated shoots (fig. 9.2).

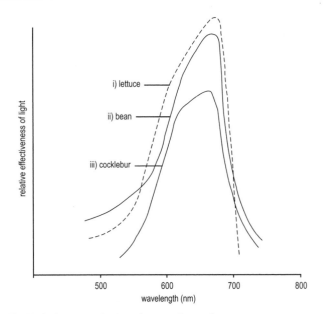

Fig. 9.2: Action spectra for three photo morphogenetic responses

i)   promotion of lettuce seed germination

ii) hypocotyl hook opening in etiolated bean seedlings

iii) inhibition of flowering of cocklebur by means of a single light break during
     nights that would be sufficiently long to induce flowering

What pigment?

The first step in any light initiated process is the absorption of
light energy by a pigment or **photoreceptor**. Because the most
effective type of light for photomorphogenesis is red light the
pigment involved must be one that absorbs more light energy
from red light than from any other colour. We would expect it
to be a blue green pigment, a bit like chlorophyll.

> ### Key point
> The pigment in question was discovered in the 1950's and
> purified in the following decade. It is called **phytochrome**.

Photoreversibility

One very characteristic feature of responses mediated by
phytochrome is that, just as they can be switched on by red

light, they can be switched off by light of longer wavelengths of between about 700 and 750 nm. Light of these wavelengths is known as **far red** light. The phenomenon of a promoting effect of red light associated with an inhibitory effect of far red light is an example of **photoreversibility** and is sufficient evidence, by itself, that phytochrome is involved.

The first demonstration of photoreversibility in this context came from a study of light induced germination of lettuce seeds made by Harry Borthwick and Sterling Hendricks in 1952. Their results can be summarised as follows:

- in permanent darkness up to a maximum of 20% of seeds germinated (the control)
- when given a 1 min. exposure to red light (wavelength 666 nm) and then returned to darkness, nearly all the seeds germinated
- when given a four minute exposure to far red light (wavelength 730 nm) and then returned to darkness, very few seeds germinated (less than 20%)
- when given 1 min. of red light, followed immediately by the far red light exposure, up to a maximum of about 20% of seeds germinated (i.e. the same as the control)
- red light treatment given immediately after far red light caused most seeds to germinate
- whatever combination of red and far red light was given, the result depended only on the last type of light the seeds were exposed to - if it was red then germination was high; if it was far red, germination was low.

> **Key point**
> Phytochrome controlled plant responses are photo-reversible: red light initiates, far red light inhibits.

The nature and properties of phytochrome

Photoreversibility is due to the fact that phytochrome exists in two interchangeable forms, the red absorbing form and the far red absorbing form. When either form absorbs enough light energy of the appropriate wavelength it is rapidly converted to the other.

> **Key point**
>
> Pr - absorbs red light - converted to Pfr - absorbs far red light – converted to Pr .... etc.
>
> **Pr** = red absorbing form of phytochrome (also called P_{660})
>
> **Pfr** = far red absorbing form of phytochrome (also called P_{730})

The phytochrome system is so sensitive that the conversion of one form of phytochrome to the other requires periods of light of normal daylight intensity of as little as a few seconds. This emphasises the concept of phytochrome being just a switch for a change in development and not a harvester of light energy used in a quantitative way.

Although red light is most effective in turning the switch on, normal daylight also converts Pr to Pfr.

Phytochrome has the following features:

- it is a protein attached to a light absorbing molecule
- a purified preparation of the Pr form is blue-green and of the Pfr form, olive-green
- levels of phytochrome in plant tissues are very low and about 100 times lower in light grown shoots than in dark grown ones
- phytochrome is believed to be synthesised as the Pr form; no Pfr can be synthesised in darkness
- Pfr is relatively unstable, with a half life of not much longer than an hour; it's rate of degradation is about 100 times that of the Pr form, which is relatively stable but still gets degraded to a certain extent
- The Pfr form of phytochrome is considered to be the active one, i.e. the one that initiates the sequence of events resulting in developmental responses

How does phytochrome work?

As little or even less is known about how phytochrome instigates the sequence of reactions involved in large scale developmental changes as how plant hormones do the same job. It might well be the case that phytochrome

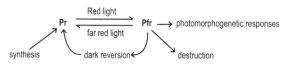

Fig. 9.3: Summary of some transformations of phytochrome

responses themselves are mediated through the production of plant growth substances. For example, seeds that require light to germinate can often be made to germinate in the dark by application of gibberellic acid, suggesting that when phytochrome acts as the photoreceptor for light in germination, it operates indirectly by causing the synthesis of gibberellins.

Despite the fact that phytochrome is not generally found to be a membrane associated protein, it can act rapidly by causing redistribution of ions across cellular membranes. This is the case in some photonastic movements (see Ch. 7).

It is also thought that the active form of phytochrome, Pfr, can switch on gene and enzyme action. Many enzymes are regulated through the action of phytochrome and some genes are controlled by phytochrome, among them the gene associated with the synthesis of one of the units of the photosynthetic enzyme, rubisco (see Ch. 2). How phytochrome might control gene expression, however, is not clear.

More than one phytochrome

There are now thought to be two, or even more than two, varieties of phytochrome. They differ in having slightly different red light absorption peaks but otherwise behave in essentially the same way. The more familiar P_{660} type is referred to as **Type 1** and is the predominant one found in etiolated seedlings while **Type 2** phytochrome is more typical of green plants and seeds and has an absorption peak of 654 nm.

Amounts of light

Most phytochrome responses require only a very short exposure to light and are fully implemented by as little as one percent of the energy in one minute of full sunlight. There are, however, other responses that require longer periods of light and show a peak of activity that differs from the typical 660 – 670 nm wavelengths. For example, the synthesis of the purple pigments, anthocyanins, in dark grown seedlings is initiated by the classic red far/red reversible phytochrome mechanism, but continued light is required for full development of the colour. The most effective light for this longer term reaction is nearer the far red part of the spectrum. Such reactions to prolonged light are referred to as **high irradiance reactions** (**HIR's**). They rely on phytochrome but do not show photoreversibility.

There are also believed to be phytochrome responses that are a hundred times or so more sensitive than the familiar red/far red reactions. For example, very low levels of red light can increase the subsequent phototropic sensitivity of cereal coleoptiles even though no measurable conversion of Pr to Pfr can be detected. Responses of this sort are called **very low fluence responses** (**VLFR's**).

The role of phytochrome in the natural environment

It is easy to see the advantage to a plant of being able to respond to light by means of the red light absorbing form of phytochrome. Sun light contains a lot of energy in the red part of the spectrum and is effective in bringing about photomorphogenetic effects. Sunlight might just as well be red light as far as the plant's red light responses are concerned. Phytochrome enables a plant to distinguish light from dark.

But how do we explain the far red light response? The answer is that green leaves filter out a lot of the red light from the sun's rays but very little of the far red. It is by means of the far red absorbing form of phytochrome that a plant is able to distinguish this filtered sunlight, from which photosynthetically useful wavelengths have been removed, from normal sunlight. A light sensitive seed, for example, will not germinate under a leaf canopy because the ratio of far red-to-red light is too high. It is thereby prevented from germinating into an environment deprived of utilisable light.

Key point
Phytochrome not only tells a plant whether it is dark or light but also gives it information about the quality and usefulness of the light.

Other pigments

Photomorphogenesis, photoreversibility and phytochrome have become almost synonymous. Other photoreceptors, however, exist in plants and may be involved in photomorphogenetic responses. Cryptochrome (see p. 86) is a good example. It is involved in phototropism and also, probably, in seed germination, de-etiolation and anthocyanin production.

Photoperiodism

The term, **photoperiodism**, applies to the variation in day and night-length throughout the year, the sensing of changes in day-length by plants and their responses to those changes. Day-length has effects on almost every aspect of plant growth, for example: germination, dormancy and renewed growth, stem elongation, rooting, stem branching, tillering of grasses, formation of storage organs, senescence, leaf fall and, most notably on account of the amount of research that has been done to try to understand it - flowering.

Photoperiodism is important in the management of a plant's development because the length of the day, and whether successive days are getting longer or shorter, offer the most accurate and reliable clues to the season.

Key point
The lives of plants are attuned to the seasons primarily by means of sensitivity to daylength.

Photoperiodism and phytochrome

Photoperiodism involves more than just the detection of light. It also requires either measurement of the length of time for which a plant is exposed to light and to darkness, or an indication of the timing of a light stimulus in relation to an internal clock. In all cases that have been studied, it is phytochrome that is the primary light detector. Light responses in photoperiodic events, therefore, show the typical red/far red reversibility and expected action spectra for phytochrome.

Flowering and photoperiodism

From here on we shall consider only flowering as an example of a photoperiodically controlled process, though many of the principles apply to other aspects of growth and development that are affected by day-length.

Types of plant

Different plants are affected very differently in their flowering behaviour by day-length. Some, such as the tomato, are not affected very much at all. They are **day - neutral** or **indeterminate**, that is they flower when they are old enough to do so, irrespective of the day-length. In any case the effect of daylength on flowering does not happen in isolation and other factors are almost always involved: the age of the plant, its exact variety, its nutritional status, the temperature at which it grows and the intensity and quality of its illumination. Consequently the requirements for flowering in different plants and the conditions that promote flowering can be extremely complex. To keep things simple we shall concentrate on two types of plant, obligate **short day plants** and obligate **long day plants**. 'Obligate' signifies the **necessity** for short or long days. The plants will not flower without them. Alternative terms for the same classes of plants are '**qualitative**' and '**absolute**' short or long day plants.

Short day plants

> **Key point**
> A short day plant is defined as one that flowers when the day-length is shorter than a critical maximum length.

This means that a short day plant will flower as the days are getting shorter, i.e. after the longest day of the year, in the later summer and autumn. To remind yourself of this point you might like to refer to such plants as **shortening** day plants. Examples of short day plants are:

Cocklebur (*Xanthium strumarium*); critical day-length = 15.5 h.

Japanese morning glory (*Pharbitis nil*); critical day-length = 14 – 15 h.

Soybean (*Glycine max*)

Maize (*Zea mays*)

Red goose foot (*Chenopodium rubrum*)

Long day plants

> **Key point**
> A long day plant is one that flowers when the day-length is longer than a critical minimum length.

Long day plants flower as the days are getting longer, i.e. after the shortest day of the year, in the spring and early summer. They are **lengthening** day plants. Examples are:

Black henbane (*Hyoscyamus niger*); critical day-length = 11 – 12 h

Scarlet pimpernel (*Anagalis arvensis*); critical day-length = 12 – 12.5 h.

Radish (*Raphanus sativus*)

Spinach (*Spinacia oleracea*)

Dill (*Anethum graveolens*)

> **Study tip**
> The examples of critical day-lengths quoted for short day plants are actually **longer** than the two for long day plants! This reinforces the point that what is important is whether the days are longer or shorter than the critical length, not their absolute length.

How do plants measure daylength?

This is a question that has motivated a very large amount of research without being unequivocally answered. Several possibilities exist:

- the daylength itself is the thing that is measured
- the length of night is what is measured, bearing in mind that in natural conditions day and night always add up to 24 hours.
- the ratio of day and night lengths is what is important
- the timing of light is the key; i.e. whether it is light or dark at a certain time or at certain times during a 24 h cycle; this idea presupposes some internal measurement of time on the part of the plant.

One thing to bear in mind in relation to these and alternative ideas is that because phytochrome detects light in photoperiodism, it doesn't follow that it can also measure the length of periods of light.

Experimental evidence

In nature, of course, every cycle of light followed by darkness is exactly 24 hours long. Under experimental conditions, however, plants can be given any combination of light and dark periods. This widens the scope for experiment immensely but has also led to a baffling amount of information that often confuses as much as clarifies.

General conclusions

> **Key point**
> Flowering in daylength sensitive plants cannot be explained on the basis of daylength alone, nor nightlength, nor the ratio of the lengths of day and night.

Rhythmic phenomena

Fig. 9.4 shows the results of an experiment using the short day plant soybean (critical daylength = 14 h). What becomes evident from this experiment is that, underlying

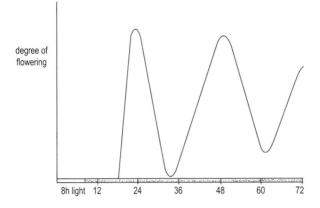

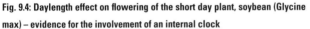

Fig. 9.4: Daylength effect on flowering of the short day plant, soybean (Glycine max) – evidence for the involvement of an internal clock
The graph shows the degree of flowering for groups of plants kept under different regimes of light and dark. All plants received 7 cycles of 8 h of light in combination with varying dark periods of up to 64 h. When the total cycle length (light + dark) was 24 h, 48 h or 72 h flowering was promoted most. With cycle lengths of 18 h, 34 h and 60 h flowering was nil or very low. (Data from Hamner, 1963)

the response to light in photoperiodism, is the plant's own internal rhythm or clock. All living organisms show clock like rhythms that continue in the absence of external stimuli, e.g. leaf movements (see Ch. 7). When the periodicity of such internal clocks is 24 hours the rhythm is called a **circadian** rhythm.

Keypoint
In many cases, if not all, a circadian rhythm linked to the phytochrome system is the only satisfactory way to explain photoperiodic events.

123

Tutorial

Progress questions

1. What is photomorphogenesis?
2. Summarise the characteristics of phytochrome.
3. Give some examples of photomorphogenesis controlled by phytochrome.
4. What are 'high irradiance reactions' and 'very low fluence responses'?
5. What is photoperiodism? Give some examples of photoperiodic phenomena in plants.
6. What are i) day neutral ii) long day iii) short day plants?

Seminar discussion

1. To what extent are plants attuned to the quality, quantity and periodicity of light in their environment? What information is conveyed to a plant in the light that it receives?

Practical assignments

1. Grow two lots of the same type of seed (e.g. peas or broad beans), one in total darkness and the other in a good light. Record the differences between the seedlings. Also record the changes that occur to the dark grown seedlings after they are brought into the light. What are these changes called?
2. Read about all the experiments that have been done in an attempt to understand the photoperiodic control of flowering and try to summarise the conclusions.

Study tips

1. The design of some experiments in plant physiology, especially those involving varying light and dark periods (e.g. fig. 9.4) is extremely complicated. You must first understand exactly how an experiment was set up and why it was done that way. Until you do - don't try to interpret the results - don't even look at them.

10 Correlations

One-minute overview

The growth and development of different parts of a plant are closely correlated. There are also correlations between the growth and development of the whole plant and environmental factors, particularly seasonal changes. Both types of correlation are essential for the successful completion of a plant's life cycle and for its survival from year to year. Correlations are effected by a complex combination of environmental and internal signals but invariably involve communication by means of plant growth substances.

In this chapter you will learn about:
- the significance of correlations
- internal and external correlations
- apical dominance and its control
- senescence
- low temperature effects

Introduction

A plant consists of many separate parts, each of which might be thought to be growing and developing independently of the others. The roots, for example, grow downwards and outwards in the soil while the shoot develops in a completely different environment and in the opposite direction. The different parts of a plant, however, are far from independent. The growth and activity of one part invariably affects that of other parts.

Key point
Interactions between the various parts of a plant are referred to as **growth correlations**.

125

An example of a growth correlation is the reduction of shoot growth by restriction of root growth. Fruit trees are sometimes grown in containers to limit the growth of their roots and, in turn to prevent the tree itself becoming too vigorous. Root restriction tends to encourage the production of fruit. Root pruning is another recognised way of bringing unproductive fruit trees into fruit.

Causes of correlations

In the above example at least part of the cause is easy to see. Roots supply mineral nutrients and water to the shoot. If the roots are restricted, the supply of these essentials is reduced and the growth of the shoot is less vigorous. Equally, if the shoots and leaves of a plant are stopped from growing vigorously, or are starved of light, the roots will suffer through lack of photoassimilates.

But how is the effect of root restriction, or root and shoot pruning on fruit production explained? For these types of correlative effect we need less obvious explanations, such as hormonal communication or competition between different parts of the plant for available resources.

Internal and external correlations

There are two types of correlation:

- internal correlations are those, like the examples above, which involve the influence of one part of a plant on another and are controlled solely by internal factors.
- external correlations are correlations between the growth and development of a plant and some environmental, often seasonal, factor or factors.

The correlation between flowering and daylength (Ch. 9) is a good example of the second of these two types. External correlations, although they involve external stimuli, are still controlled by a plant's internal physiological mechanisms. Most aspects of plant growth and development involve an inseparable combination of external and internal correlations.

Apical dominance

A good example of a predominantly internal correlation (though external factors can enter the equation) is that of shoot **apical dominance** (fig. 10.1).

> **Key point**
> Apical dominance is, quite literally, the dominance in growth of the apical shoot of a plant over the axillary (side) shoots.
>
> **Study tip**
> **Axillary** buds are so called because they are formed in the axils of leaves. They are **not** *auxiliary* buds, though, ironically, they do have an auxiliary function!

Degrees of shoot apical dominance

If every bud of a plant grew to the same extent and in the same direction the result would be a dense mass of shoots all trying to occupy the same space.

The degree of apical dominance can vary from complete, in which case the axillary buds do not grow at all, to moderate,

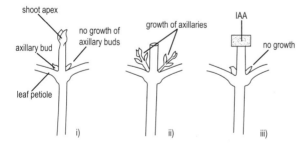

Fig. 10.1: Apical dominance and the role of auxin

i) growing shoot apex inhibits the axillary buds = complete apical dominance

ii) when the shoot apex is cut off the axillary buds start to grow almost immediately

iii) inhibition of axillary buds can be maintained by replacing the shoot apex with a high concentration of IAA.

where the side shoots grow less in length than the main shoot and at an angle rather than vertically. Younger plants are more likely to show complete apical dominance. Axillary buds nearer the shoot apex are more likely to be completely inhibited than are lower buds. Different species of plant show different degrees of apical dominance.

> **Key point**
> Apical dominance ensures that plants take on a spreading form that makes more efficient use of the available light or, in the early stages of growth, enables the young shoot to gain height quickly without putting unnecessary resources into producing side shoots.

How is apical dominance controlled?

There are really two questions here:

i) why, in the case of complete apical dominance, do the axillary buds not grow?
ii) how does the apex exert this control over the axillary buds?

Neither question has been answered with any degree of certainty. The second question is even more difficult to answer than the first.

In considering the following possible answers to these questions (for all of which there is good evidence) be aware that:

i) the answers may well involve a combination of things, i.e. more than one possibility may be right and
ii) the answers may be different for different species and in different situations.

1. Why the buds don't grow

- they contain high levels of an inhibitor: the inhibitor is almost definitely not auxin, despite the fact that inhibition by auxin may seem to be the most obvious explanation of the experimental evidence (see fig. 10.1); abscisic acid is a good candidate for the role of inhibitor

- they are not supplied with adequate nutrients, either because the growing shoot tip takes the lion's share or because the flow of nutrients is diverted away from them
- they contain inadequate levels of plant growth substances: cytokin is one and, ironically, auxin may be another.

2. The role of the apex

- auxin, produced in the growing shoot tip, in moving down towards the axillary buds acts as the message and agent of inhibition; it is not the inhibitor itself but acts indirectly in a way that is not understood
- the growing apex is a direct competitor for nutrients and growth substances supplied by the rest of the plant
- the apex, or auxin alone, controls the transport of nutrients and growth substances such that they do not reach the axillary buds
- the apex, or apex-produced auxin alone, controls the synthesis of plant growth substances in the axillary buds, again by an unknown mechanism.

Senescence

A number of correlations in plants involve the decline and death of one part while other parts remain viable. The process leading to the eventual death of part of a living plant is referred to as **senescence** (literally 'growing old'). When tissues senesce, their proteins and other macromolecules are broken down and the products are exported to other parts of the plant. Leaf senescence, for example is accompanied by the breakdown of chlorophyll, the yellowing of the leaf and the loss of up to 50% of the dry weight.

Key point
Senescence is not simply death but is a living process that is as much an adaptive part of the life of a plant as synthesis and growth.

Senescence is a necessary part of a plant's life cycle and often there is a sequence of senescence as different structures play their part and others take over. For example, once fertilisation of the ovules has been achieved, the petals, style and anthers of a flower begin to senesce and, at the same time, the seeds and fruit start to develop. To show that this sequence is a true correlation it is only necessary to prevent pollination and observe that senescence of the flower is delayed.

Senescence and seasonal stimuli

Senescence is often initiated by external signals that give a clue to the seasons. Daylength and temperature are two such signals. Leaves of deciduous trees, for example, senesce and fall off in response to decreasing daylength (see Ch. 8 – photoperiodism). Leaf fall illustrates well the distinction between senescence and death. If a tree in leaf is killed, or a branch cut off, the leaves shrivel and go brown but don't fall. Proper leaf fall requires the production of an abscission layer at the base of the leaf stalk and this process can only be started when the leaf is caused to senesce by the appropriate stimulus. So we have:

stimulus (daylength) → internal signal → senescence of leaf → leaf abscision

In a large number of perennial plants all the aerial parts senesce at the end of the season, leaving only an underground perennating organ, such as a bulb or corm, to survive the winter.

Control of senescence

When a leaf is removed from a plant it starts to senesce. This suggests that influences coming from other parts of the plant are necessary to prevent senescence of leaves in the intact plant. One such influence that is known to be involved is cytokinin.

- applied cytokinin can prevent the senescence of detached leaves or leaves that are about to senesce naturally
- there is a reduction in the supply of cytokinins from the roots to the leaves at the onset of natural leaf senescence

- if a leaf is cut from a plant and treated with auxin to encourage root formation it does not senesce because the new roots supply it with cytokinin
- cytokinins cause the movement of nutrients towards parts where the cytokinins are in relatively high concentration (i.e. away from senescing tissues and into younger tissues)
- cytokinins may act by preventing the breakdown of cell membranes.

> **Key point**
> Senescence, and correlations involving senescence of some parts of a plant and growth of others, are, at least in part, controlled by the supply and distribution of cytokinins.

Initiation of senescence

More is known about how senescence can be slowed down or prevented than about how it is started. Nevertheless we can say that:

- ethene, abscisic acid and lack of cytokinin can all bring about premature senescence
- senescence is genetically programmed into each species
- age is, therefore, the prime initiator of senescence
- external factors such as reduced light intensity, daylength, water stress and nutrient status can initiate or speed up senescence
- correlations play a big part: flower and fruit development in annual plants can be a signal for leaf senescence; older leaves are more likely to senesce in the presence of younger, developing leaves
- the mechanism behind these sorts of correlation is unclear.

Seasonal correlations due to temperature

Although changing daylength is the best clue to the time of year, temperatures are also indicative of the seasons.

> **Key point**
> A number of seasonally correlated plant responses are brought about by exposure to low temperatures.

Low temperatures can either signify the onset of autumn or winter or, if they are prolonged, can indicate to a plant that winter is passing and spring is near. There are, therefore, two types of responses to cold: those that prepare a plant for winter and those that start it developing again in the spring. Examples of the first would be the onset of dormancy in buds, seeds and underground storage organs and, of the latter, the breaking of dormancy. Paradoxically, lowered temperatures can have exactly opposite effects on the same organs at different times and in different circumstances.

Positive effects

Low temperatures can have a positive effect (i.e. promotion) on at least five aspects of plant development – providing:

i) the temperature is below a certain minimum that varies for different species but would typically be in the range 0° to 10°C.

ii) temperatures in this range persist for a minimum length of time, usually 1 to 10 weeks, again depending on species and response.

Aspects of development promoted by prolonged cold

- flowering of 'winter' annuals and biennials – low temperature induction of flowering is known as **vernalisation**
- seed germination – breaking seed dormancy by cold treatment is called **stratification** or **pre-chilling**
- breaking of dormancy of buds of deciduous woody perennials
- development of underground storage organs such as tubers, corms and bulbs
- vegetative growth and development of form.

How do low temperatures work?

The mechanism of low temperature effects is largely unknown. It is a particular puzzle because metabolism is invariably speeded up by **increasing** temperature, and for lowered temperatures to promote aspects of growth and development seems to contradict this general principle. What is known is that:

- the reception of the cold stimulus and the response usually occur in the same place (e.g. a dormant bud)
- plant hormones, especially gibberellins, can often substitute for low temperatures and, for example, cause seeds to germinate or biennials to flower in the absence of a cold treatment
- the processes initiated by low temperatures can sometimes be reversed by subsequent higher temperatures
- responses to cold are usually delayed, that is, they do not occur during the cold period but some time afterwards
- low temperatures often interact with other factors such as daylength in their effects
- effects generally depend on the degree of cold and the length of time it lasts; for example 50% of apple seeds stored for 4 weeks at 4°C will subsequently germinate but, if they remain at that temperature for more than 8 weeks, nearly 100% will germinate.

Tutorial

Progress questions

1. What is meant by a growth correlation?
2. What is apical dominance? How does it benefit a plant?
3. Summarise the role of auxin, inhibitors and cytokinin in the control of apical dominance.
4. Give examples of correlations involving the development of parts of a plant and the associated senescence of other parts.

Seminar discussion

1. In what ways are growth correlations essential for the efficient growth, development and ultimate survival of a plant?
2. How do plants prepare for the coming season?

Practical assignments

1. Record the growth and senescence of the different parts of a single plant during the season. A pot grown bulb e.g. daffodil, tulip or *Hippeastrum* would be a good choice.
2. Find out what you can about the control of leaf senescence and leaf abscission. This is a well-researched and documented phenomenon in plant physiology.

Study tips

1. The control of correlations is one of the least well-understood areas of plant physiology. Bear this in mind in your reading.
2. Make sure you know how to mind map and mind map this chapter and all of the chapters in this book.

11 **Seed Germination**

One-minute overview

A seed is a quiescent stage in the life cycle that allows for dispersal of a plant species in both space and time. Germination is the dramatic resumption of growth of the seed when conditions become suitable. Conditions favourable for germination include a distinct range of temperatures, the presence of water and oxygen and, in many cases, light. Seeds that don't germinate even when conditions appear to be suitable are referred to as dormant. Germination starts with the absorption of water, followed by the growth of the embryo and the mobilisation of food reserves and ends with the establishment of the seedling.

In this chapter you will learn about:
- seed structure
- quiescence and dormancy
- stages in germination
- conditions for germination
- special requirements for germination of some seeds

What is a seed?

Key point

All seeds consists of three basic parts:
- embryo
- food reserve
- protective coat

A seed is a genetic mosaic of maternal tissue and tissue formed by fertilisation. The embryo is, in most cases, the product of fertilisation, and contains both paternal and maternal genes while the seed coat is of maternal origin only. The food reserve is usually a product of fertilisation but can,

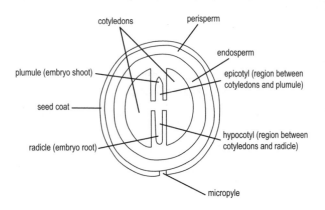

Fig. 11.1: The structure of a dicotyledonous seed

  i)   cotyledons may be the major food reserve of the seed (e.g. peas and beans) or may have no food storage function

 ii)   all flowering plant seeds have endosperm immediately after fertilisation; it may develop to become a major food reserve or it may have disappeared by the time the seed is fully mature

iii)   perisperm is an uncommon food reserve formed from maternal ovular tissue

 iv)   the seed coat or testa of different types of seed varies from thin and papery to very thick and very hard

  v)   the micropyle is a pore in the seed coat which, in some cases, aids water absorption.

in some species, be maternal tissue only. Cotyledons, for example, which form the food reserve in peas and beans, are part of the embryo; endosperm, the food reserve in cereal grains and many oily seeds, is a product of the additional fusion of nuclei (additional, that is, to the fusion of nuclei producing the zygote) that is a feature of the fertilisation process in flowering plants. Endosperm is **triploid** tissue, containing paternal genes and a double helping of maternal genes. Occasionally cells that were part of the unfertilised ovule and, therefore, maternal in origin, develop into a food storage tissue (e.g. **perisperm**).

Is a seed living?

The fact that seeds can have a water content well below that of normal plant tissues (down to 5% or less) and no discernible respiration or metabolism does not mean they are not living. The state of a dry seed is described as **quiescent**. It is inactive but retains the potential for germination and growth. Quiescence and dormancy are not the same and you should be clear about the difference.

> *Key point*
>
> A seed is quiescent mainly because it has not absorbed water and cannot grow for that reason. A dormant seed, on the other hand, can be fully hydrated and, even when it appears to have all it needs to germinate, it still won't do so.

Seed longevity

Seeds can remain quiescent in a dry state for long periods of time. How long seeds remain viable depends on the species and the conditions in which they are kept. The drier a seed is, the longer it will remain viable. Low temperature and high carbon dioxide concentrations also prolong the life of a seed. It is quite common for seeds to germinate after up to 30 years storage and there are documented cases of seeds remaining viable for well over 100 years. Beyond this age it is hard to date seeds with any certainty, but it is believed that some seeds that have germinated could have been 500 or even 1,000 years old.

Stages in germination

Germination is a process that is switched on by a combination of internal controls and the right environmental conditions. The exact starting point is difficult to define. For counting and recording purposes a seed is usually said to have germinated at the first sign of the radicle or shoot emerging through the seed coat. Because germination leads into the continuous development of the seedling there is no point at which it can be said to have finished and normal growth to have begun. Perhaps the best criterion for the completion of germination is the onset of photosynthesis and the loss of dependence of the seedling on the food reserves of the seed.

Water uptake

Key point
The first stage in germination, though it does not, by itself, inevitably result in germination (see dormancy), is the uptake of water.

The process is referred to as **imbibition** and leads to the hydration of the tissues of the seed.

Because a seed is dry there is, initially at any rate, no osmotic uptake of water. Water is attracted by adsorption to colloidal molecules such as proteins and cell wall polysaccharides. The forces involved are matric forces (see Ch. 1) and can be quite huge. Seed matric potentials can have negative values of hundreds of bars. The positive result of these forces is an imbibition pressure that is often responsible for the splitting of the seed coat, prior to the emergence of the radicle or shoot.

Water uptake is usually rapid and substantial. A pea, for example, at room temperature, will absorb twice its own weight of water in about 8 hours.

Onset of metabolism

Key point
Once a seed is fully hydrated, enzymes can operate, food reserves can be broken down, soluble products can be moved about and respiration can start.

Respiration

The first sign, after the uptake of water that germination is commencing is the onset of respiration. Carbon dioxide is produced and, in the case of aerobic respiration, oxygen is consumed. Initially the respiratory quotient (see Ch. 3) may be high because the seed coat acts as a barrier to the diffusion of oxygen. If the food reserve being respired is oil or fat the respiratory quotient will be lower than if it is carbohydrate.

Mobilisation of food reserves

The growing parts of a seed need to be supplied with materials and respiratory substrates from the reserves stored in the cotyledons, endosperm or other tissues. This involves:

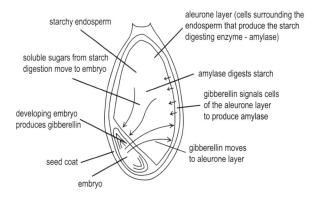

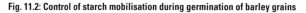

Fig. 11.2: Control of starch mobilisation during germination of barley grains

  i) enzymatic breakdown of insoluble food reserve materials to soluble products,

 ii) transport of these soluble materials to the developing parts of the embryo and

iii) their use as substrates for respiration and synthesis reactions. The control of these processes has been well studied in barley grains.

A hormonal signal coordinates the embryo's nutrient requirements with their provision from the food storage tissue, the hormone (gibberellin) acting at the level of enzyme synthesis (see fig. 11.2).

Growth of root and shoot

> **Key point**
> Usually it is the radicle that is the first structure to emerge through the seed coat, though in some seeds (e.g. saltworts, *Salsola*) it is the shoot.

There is nothing unusual about the extension growth, whether of radicle or shoot, that occurs during germination. It is affected in the same way as all growth by external factors such as temperature, pH and water availability and requires the same nutrients.

A seed can exhibit one of two types of germination. Which type any particular species shows depends on precisely which cells of the embryo elongate most rapidly.

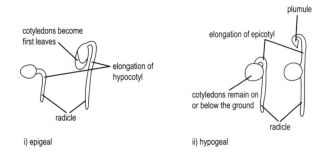

Fig. 11.3: Epigeal and hypogeal germination

The two types of germination are:

- **epigeal**
- **hypogeal**

Epigeal germination

- the region of the embryo that elongates most rapidly is the **hypocotyl** (see figs. 11.1 & 11.3)
- the seed is raised above the ground by elongation of the hypocotyl
- the cotyledons usually become the first photosynthetic structures
- seeds with epigeal germination tend to be small.

Hypogeal germination

- the regions that elongates most rapidly are the radicle itself and the epicotyl
- the seed and its cotyledon(s) remain below or on the surface of the ground
- large seeds usually have hypogeal germination.

Very early in the germination process the normal tropic responses of root and shoot are established. The root grows downwards and the shoot grows upwards and towards the light.

Tutorial

Progress Questions

1. Name the three basic parts of a seed.
2. What is the function of a cotyledon?
3. After the uptake of water what is the first sign that germination is commencing, what gas is consumed and what gas is produced?
4. What is the first structure to emerge through the seed coat?
5. What are the two types of germination?

Seminar Discussion

Green issues are becoming more important in the political arena. What role do plant physiologists have in explaining the role of this area in science to the public?

> **Study tip**
>
> To remember which type of germination is which: *epi* means **on** and *hypo* means **under**; hence epigeal - on the ground and hypogeal – under the ground. Do not be confused by the fact that in **epi**geal germination it is the **hypo**cotyl that elongates and when the **epi**cotyl elongates we get **hypo**geal germination! It is the exact opposite of what you might expect.

12 Seed Germination (2)

One-minute overview

Plants will only grow effectively when there are good conditions for germination. In this chapter we will continue and build on the work started in the last chapter.

In this chapter you will learn:
- the conditions for germination.
- gases
- temperature
- mineral salts and light
- seed dormancy

Conditions for germination

Water

> *Key point*
> All seeds need water for germination.

The same principles as were encountered in Ch. 1 apply to the uptake of water by seeds. As long as the water potential of a seed is lower than that of its surroundings the seed will absorb water. It takes extreme environmental conditions, very dry soil or high concentrations of solutes (e.g. in saline soils), to make water unavailable. As was pointed out before, the water potentials of dry seeds can be very low indeed.

Gases

> *Key point*
> Generally, seeds need oxygen to germinate fully.

Very few species – rice is one – can germinate totally anaerobically though germination of a lot of seeds may proceed to some degree in the absence of oxygen. In the early stages of germination, oxygen is often in short supply because the seed coat and the tissues of the seed constitute a considerable barrier to the diffusion of oxygen into the seed.

Carbon dioxide tends to inhibit germination and is an important factor affecting germination in the soil environment. The combined effects of oxygen and carbon dioxide on germination, however, are very confusing, largely because:

- concentrations inside a seed are very hard to determine
- oxygen and carbon dioxide concentrations are usually inversely related
- different species react differently; there are exceptions to any generalisation
- different rules apply at different stages of germination.

In the soil environment another gas of significance is ethene. Ethene is known to stimulate the germination of some seeds under certain circumstances, though, again, few clear conclusions can be drawn.

Temperature

Key point
For every type of seed there is a range of temperatures within which, given all other necessary conditions, it will germinate.

The limits of the range differ from species to species. Within the range there is an optimum temperature for germination (or, more correctly, two optima, one for percentage germination and the other for rate of germination). For example, oats germinate most successfully (i.e. reaching a higher percentage germination) at about 15°C but do so more slowly than at higher temperatures. Some examples are given in Table 12.1.

Some seeds germinate most successfully when the temperature fluctuates between daytime and night. A diurnal alternation of cooler and warmer temperatures is a good indication that a seed is near the surface of the ground and in an advantageous position to germinate.

The special case of a cold requirement for germination was discussed in Ch. 9. (see stratification).

Species	Minimum °C	Optimum °C	Maximum °C
Wheat	3 – 5	15 – 31	30 – 43
Barley	3 – 5	19 – 27	30 – 40
Oats	3 – 5	25 – 31	30 – 40
Maize	8 – 10	32 – 35	40 - 44
Melon	16 – 19	30 – 40	45 – 50

Table 12.1: Temperature ranges for germination of different seeds

Mineral salts and pH

Germination is affected by the soil solution, its mineral composition and its pH. For example:

- pH can affect the imbibition of seeds, due to its effect on the structure of seed proteins
- toxic ions such as heavy metals can inhibit germination, especially the growth of the radicle and the shoot
- very high concentrations of ions can make water less available
- nitrates are known to stimulate the germination of some seeds.

Light

Key point

It is a common but erroneous belief that seeds germinate best in the dark. Actually, light favours the germination of a lot more species of seeds than does darkness.

The responses of seeds to light range from those that must have a light stimulus before they will germinate to those that germinate better in the light and from these to a few that are completely prevented from germinating by light. The topic of light induced germination was covered in Ch. 8.

Seed dormancy

Key point

Dormancy in seeds is the inability to germinate even when the seed is supplied with water and kept at a suitable temperature in a normal atmosphere.

Causes of dormancy

Impermeable seed coat

A hard seed coat can prevent the passage of water and oxygen into the seed or can simply restrain the growth of the embryo. It could be argued that an impermeable seed coat merely extends the quiescence of a seed and that the seed is not truly physiologically dormant. Some support for this argument comes from the observation that removing or damaging the seed coat can often bring about normal germination. Scratching or otherwise abrading the seed coat to make a seed germinate is known as **scarification**.

Immaturity of embryo

When a seed is shed from the parent plant the embryo is not necessarily mature enough to play its part in germination immediately. A certain period of time, known as **after-ripening** is required before the seed is ready to germinate.

Inhibitors

Dormancy is often associated with the presence of inhibitors in the seed or the fruit. Abscisic acid is one such inhibitor but a wide variety of organic compounds can also be involved. Dormancy is broken as soon as the levels of the inhibitor drops below a certain level.

Water can dissolve away inhibitors, especially if they are located in the seed coat, and, in some species germination will only happen after enough rain has fallen to leach out all the inhibitor. This is a particularly useful adaptation for desert plants, making sure they do not germinate at the first drop of rain, only to dry up soon afterwards. Seeds of fleshy fruits such as tomatoes are dormant inside the fruit for two reasons: the presence of inhibitors and the low osmotic potential of the juice of the fruit.

Special requirements

Dormancy can often be broken by stimuli such as light, cold treatment suitable photoperiods or alternating higher and lower temperatures. One cause of dormancy, therefore, is simply the absence of the necessary specific stimulus. Some seeds can be extremely demanding in their germination requirements.

Breaking of dormancy by specific stimuli is likely to be achieved through an effect on levels of inhibitors and other growth substances within the seed.

Secondary or induced dormancy

Seeds may be dormant from the moment they are shed. This is **primary dormancy**. Or they may be able to germinate when they are first produced and become dormant at a later stage. This is called **secondary dormancy**.

Secondary dormancy may be induced by environmental conditions. Lettuce seeds, for example, will germinate in the light as soon as they are formed. If they are kept, imbibed, in the dark at a high temperature they will no longer germinate even when returned to the conditions under which similar seeds germinated before. Only treatments such as chilling or adding gibberellin will make them germinate. Burial is often a cause of secondary dormancy, ensuring that seeds do not germinate unless they are sufficiently close to the surface for seedling establishment.

Tutorial

Progress questions

1. Distinguish between quiescence and dormancy of a seed.
2. What are the possible causes of seed dormancy?
3. What conditions are needed for the germination of: i) all seeds ii) seeds of particular species?

Seminar discussion

Discuss the ecological significance and survival value of:
  i) epigeal and hypogeal germination
 ii) light requirement for germination
iii) primary and secondary dormancy
iv) water soluble inhibitors in seed dormancy.

Practical assignments

1. Find a glass bottle with flat sides and a narrow neck. An old style medicine bottle is ideal. Fill it with dry peas and immerse in a bowl of water. The force generated as the peas absorb water is usually enough to crack the glass. The bottle is unlikely to explode but, just in case, it is sensible to cover the bowl.

2. Observe both epigeal (e.g. dwarf or French bean) and hypogeal germination (e.g. broad bean). Take careful note of exactly where growth takes place and what happens to the cotyledons of the seed as germination proceeds.

3. Set up samples of seeds for germination. Keep one sample of each species in the light and one in total darkness. Do not look at the dark sample until there are signs of germination in the light. You can then record the percentage germination in the two conditions. Good seeds to try that will show a light requirement for germination are dandelion, willowherb and foxglove.

Web sites about Plant Physiology

The internet, or world wide web, is an amazingly useful resource, giving the student nearly free and almost immediate information on any topic. Ignore this vast and valuable store of materials at your peril! The following list of web sites may be helpful for you. Please note that neither the author nor the publisher is responsible for content or opinions expressed on the sites listed, which are simply intended to offer starting points for students. Also, please remember that the internet is a fast-evolving environment, and links may come and go. If you have some favourite sites you would like to see mentioned in future editions of this book, please write to Dr Edwin Oxlade c/o Studymates (address on back cover), or email him at the address shown below. You will find a free selection of useful and readymade student links genetics, biology and other subjects at the Studymates web site. Happy surfing!

Studymates web site: *http://www.studymates.co.uk*
Edwin Oxlade email: *edwinoxlade@studymates.co.uk*

Plant Physiology

http://www.plantphysiol.org/
This is the website of the American society of plant biologists. This is worthy of your time, especially if you are aiming to be an academic.

Archive of Plant Physiology

http://www.pubmedcentral.nih.gov
This is an archive to the above site with lots of free content.

Stephen G.Saupe

http://employees.csbsju.edu/SSAUPE/

This is Dr Stephen Saube's personal site. He teaches at *College of St. Benedict/St. John's University Biology Department* and his site worthy of your attention. On the day we visited there was a lot of free stuff and the images were superb, where else can you get close up to a begonia? Well done Dr Saube, keep it up!

Plant Physiology Movie Page

http://employees.csbsju.edu/ssaupe/biol327/Lab/movie/movies.htm

Dr Saube's students have produced some great movies here, well worth a look at.

Plant Physiology Website

http://plantphys.info/

This is the home page of Dr Ros Koning. You do have to wade past the stuff on the home page (which he puts there for his own students, fair enough!) but he does have some brilliant images on the site that make plant physiology easier to understand. It really is worth your while to mine this site; he has some really good stuff on it.

Russian Journal of Plant Physiology

http://www.springerlink.com

This is a very officious looking site but there is a lot of good material on it.

Plant Physiology

http://plantphys.wsu.edu/

This is the Washington State University website. If you are in the USA, you really should know about this site.

Institute of Plant Physiology, Bulgarian Academy of Science

http://www.bio21.bas.bg/ipp/gapbfiles/content.html

Another good one for academics.

The Plant Cell

http://www.plantcell.org/
Another one from the American Society of Plant Biologists.

Malaysian Society of Plant Physiology

http://members.tripod.com/mspp/mspp.htm
We are never crazy about sites with a Tripod connection but if you are reading this in Malaysia you need to know about this society.

University of Basel Botanical Institute

http://plantbiology.unibas.ch/
Another good one for academics, we particularly liked the academic papers on the site.

Indian Agricultural Research Institute

http://www.iari.res.in/divisions/plant_physiology/

They say:
The Indian Agricultural Research Institute (IARI) is the country's premier national Institute for agricultural research, education and extension. It has served the cause of science and society with distinction through first rate research, generation of appropriate technologies and development of human resources. In fact, the Green Revolution was born in the fields of IARI and our graduates constitute the core of the quality human resource in India's agricultural research and education.

Whilst the site was a little formal for us, we think the work they are doing is excellent and we wish them well

American Society of Plant Biologists

http://www.aspb.org/education/reviews.cfm
Another one from the people mentioned above.

The Italian Society of Plant Physiology

http://web.tiscali.it/sifv/INDEX.HTML

They say:
* Il presente Statuto, approvato dall'Assemblea ordinaria della SIFV, convocata il 26 Ottobre 1989, sostituisce il precedente Statuto pubblicato sul "Giornale Botanico Italiano" Vol. 123, Supplemento n. 2: 3-5, 1989.

Finalità - Sede - Soci
Art. 1 La Società Italiana di Fisiologia Vegetale (SIFV) costituita a Milano nel Maggio 1961 ha lo scopo di far progredire lo sviluppo della Fisiologia Vegetale in Italia promuovendo la collaborazione tra quanti ne sono interessati e facilitando i contatti tra persone e associazioni italiane e straniere. La Società è una associazione scientifica senza scopo di lucro.

Art. 2 La Società di Fisiologia Vegetale ha sede in Milano presso il Dipartimento di Biologia "L. Gorini", già Istituto di Scienze Botaniche dell'Università.
Shamefully we have no Italian, sorry guys but the site does look good!

Journal of Plant Physiology

http://www.ingentaconnect.com/content/urban/271;jsessionid=1btnevrgvoxhk.victoria
Enough said.

Plant Sciences for Industry

http://biol.lancs.ac.uk/psi/

They say:
Plant Sciences for Industry recognises the needs of the agricultural, environmental and horticultural sectors of plant-based industry and had developed a distinctly focused programme of research and training opportunities in the plant sciences to meet these needs.

This is based in Lancaster in the UK and whilst they do not seem to keep the site updated, it is worth you knowing about them for future possible career development.

Sociedade Portuguesa de Fisiologia Vegetal

http://www.spfv.pt/

They say:
The Sociedade Portuguesa de Fisiologia Vegetal (SPFV) was founded in 1977 as an affiliated Society of the Sociedade Portuguesa de Bioquímica (SPB) and congregates scientists and graduate students within the area of Plant Biology, in particular, Plant Physiology, Plant Biochemistry and Plant Molecular Biology.

The main aims of SPFV are to disseminate information on this area of science and to promote/support meetings in cooperation with other Societies of Plant Science, in particular the SPB and the Sociedade Espanhola de Fisiologia Vegetal (SEFV). It also welcomes thematic scientific events, such as workshops.

The SPFV and the SEFV share three working groups, the Water Relations Group, the Plant Nutrition Group and the Post-Harvest Group.

The SPFV is affiliated with the Federation of the European Societies of Plant Physiology (FESPP).

Again this is a good one to know for post-graduates.

Links of interest in plant physiology

http://www.il-st-acad-sci.org/phytofisiol.html
It does what 'it says on the tin' (if you are not in the UK you will not understand that idiom but never mind). They give lots of links so make sure you bookmark them.

Useful links

http://www.uni-tuebingen.de/plantphys/links/links.html
On the basis that you cannot have too much of a good thing!

Arid Land Asgricultural research center

http://www.ars.usda.gov/main/site_main.htm?modecode=53-47-10-10

This is a US site hence the American spelling in the title.

They say:

The **Agricultural Research Service (ARS)** is the U.S. Department of Agriculture's chief scientific research agency. Our job is finding solutions to agricultural problems that affect Americans every day, from field to table.

If you are US based, bookmark the site.

Plant Physiology Department Moscow University

http://herba.msu.ru/departments/physiology/

Just trying for a bit of balance here. There is a lot of information but it is not the best-designed site we have ever seen.

Answers.com

http://www.answers.com/topic/plant-physiology

It could be just what you need for revision!

History of Plant Physiology

http://www.biologyreference.com/Gr-Hi/History-of-Plant-Physiology.html

Very simple, ignore the ads and read the history.

The Japanese Society of Plant Physiologists

http://www.jspp.org/eng/06intro/purposes.html

They say:

The Japanese Society of Plant Physiologists was established in 1959 to promote academic exchange in and contribute to the development of the field of plant physiology. Since then, it has developed into a comprehensive society for "the study of the functions of plants" whose membership includes researchers from such diverse fields as microbiology, biochemistry, molecular biology, cell biology, and genetics.

We liked the design on this site.

Index